The Busy Mom's Guide to Home-cooked Meals

By Erica Arndt

Copyright © 2016 Erica Made Designs, LLC
All rights reserved.

Book, Cover Design & Graphics by:
Erica Made Designs, LLC

No part of this publication may be reproduced, distributed, or transmitted in any form or by any means, including photocopying, recording, or other electronic or mechanical methods, without the prior written permission of the publisher, except in the case of brief quotations embodied in critical reviews and certain other noncommercial uses permitted by copyright law.
For permission requests, email the publisher, addressed "Attention: Permission Coordinator," at the address below.
erica@confessionsofahomeschooler.com

Additional works by this author are available at
www.confessionsofahomeschooler.com
Printed in the United States of America.

A word from me to you...

As a busy mom of four, I find meal planning a little on the stressful side. I actually enjoy cooking, however when we're busy with school and other activities, I don't always have time to run to the store, or think of something healthy and tasty for my family.

I don't know about you all, but it's really easy for me to want to run out and grab something quick when we're in between activities, or coming home late from something. But as we all know, that can get expensive, and it's really not very healthy depending on what you grab on the go.

But with just a little planning, it's easy to skip the take-out and create a variety of home-cooked meals for your family, even when you're busy like we are!

Since we don't have much time for meals each day, I try to plan ahead for breakfast, lunch, snack, and dinner on an almost daily basis. I normally like to head to the grocery store over the weekend to stock up on items we'll need each week. I've found that I spend less on groceries doing it this way because I'm only getting what I need based on my menu plan. Getting your produce weekly is also a good idea since they can spoil quickly and you don't want to be wasting food.

Once our busy week starts, it's easy to keep up on meals since they're already planned out for me. It's even nice to have snack ideas throughout the week as well. I am a creature of habit, and without a meal plan, I'll often revert to meals that are easy for me to make from memory. That's great except we end up eating the same meals all the time! So to promote a little bit of variety I find that having a monthly meal plan, ready to go, gives us a more well-rounded diet.

My hope is that this book will inspire you to make healthier home-cooked meals on a regular basis as opposed to heading out for take-out. I've also included a list of healthy snack ideas to help out as well. We often pre-pack them in serving size baggies so that when we're running out the door they're easy to grab and go.

Hopefully it not only inspires you to create meals at home, but also helps alleviate some of the stress that daily meal planning can cause! That way you can spend more time enjoying your family, and less time planning!

Happy cooking,
Erica

How to use the monthly meal planner...

This planner is a simple guide to help you keep your monthly meals organized. As you'll see each month is full of pre-planned meals for you. They're color coded and separated out so you'll only be eating the same main dish once a month. That way people don't get tired of the same meals over and over again!

You are also welcome to either use my meals as is, or use the blank monthly planner sheet found at the "Create Your Own Meal Plan" section to create your own. And of course you're always welcome to skip meals, or change the meal plan as needed based on your family's needs.

Monthly Meal Plans:

This book includes a monthly meal plan for January through December. You can either use my pre-planned menus or create your own. The monthly recipes also vary by season, so you'll have a nice variety of meals to look forward to throughout the year. I've also included a ton of healthy snack ideas as well as holiday treats!

Please note that I have not specified holidays in the monthly plans since the dates vary from year to year.

Weekly Shopping Lists:

At the top left you'll see a shopping list to use for that month. Simply turn to the shopping list for that week, check off what you already have, and then head to the store to check off the rest of your list!

There is also a blank shopping list so that you can create your own as well.

Create your own meal plan:

At the back of this book you'll find some customizable meal plan pages. I've included a blank monthly planning calendar page along with pre-printed meal labels that you can use in any way you'd like.

There are also blank color-coded meal labels so you can write your own meals in, and arrange them as desired.

Directions for customizable plan:

To make it more durable, I suggest you laminate the blank monthly sheet, and then hang it on your refrigerator. Run the meal labels through a magnetic laminate sheet (laminate on front, magnetic material on backside) and cut them apart.

I would suggest storing them in snack size baggies by category to make them easier to sort through.

You can also laminate the sheet and then place individual small magnetic stickers to the backside if you can't find magnetic lamination paper. Next just mix and match meals as you see fit!

Note: Of course if you use the "create your own plan" labels, you'll need to create your own grocery list rather than use mine!

Recipes:

There are recipes for almost all of the meals listed in my monthly meal planning sheets. You'll find those at the back of the book. All meals are listed in alphabetical order and by type to make them easy to locate.

There are a few exceptions that do not include recipes that are intuitive, things like hamburgers, or cheese and crackers for snack time. They are meals that should be fairly intuitive to make, and I didn't feel they needed a detailed explanation. However, if you find anything that you need clarification on, feel free to email me at erica@confessionsofahomeschooler.com and I'll make sure to help you as well as update the book with that recipe!

What about leftovers?

It really depends on the day as to whether or not we'll have left overs. If we do, then I'll usually save them for a night that I know will be busy during the week. If we don't have any leftovers for the week, then I just stick to my meal schedule.

Don't be afraid to skip a meal to use up some left overs! I also have a couple of meals that use left-overs from a previous night's dinner. So make sure to skim over each meal for that week!

And after all this meal planning, I do still like to take a night off here and there. So even though we have a meal planned, some nights I just dictate that it's mom's night off, and we'll do take out! It's okay to take a break and I definitely feel better about it if I've cooked the majority of the nights each week too.

Do you ever stray from your plan?

Yes! Of course, no one is perfect, and honestly some nights I just don't feel like having the meal listed. If that happens, I'll usually just rearrange the meals for the week, knowing that I can have it another day because I already have the ingredients for it. I may also just skip a meal all together due to random life circumstances. And that's fine too!

When do you go shopping?

I normally shop for the upcoming week on the previous weekend, Saturday or Sunday depending on our schedule. If it works better for you to shop another time, go for it! I know that I've shopped for pantry items for an entire month before and then just planned my produce trips weekly since those can spoil. Just do whatever works best for you, your schedule and your family!

Please note that the grocery lists for each week contain ingredients for every recipe that week. You'll want to cross off anything you may not need, as some are staple items that will last you a while. But I wanted to make sure and include them just in case you needed them!

One last word...

Whether you're busy working, homeschooling, or chauffeuring kids around, meal planning can be stressful. Most of us don't have much time to give a whole lot of thought into our meals for each day. I know I've been guilty of wishing for a genie to pop out of my pantry and have dinner ready for me many a time!

But my main concern is for the overall health of our family, and so for that reason I like to have some type of plan. That way I'm not scrambling at the last minute to come up with some delicious and healthy meal out of whatever is left in the pantry. Have you ever tried to come up with a meal using just paper towels and cereal? I have — it's called breakfast for dinner LOL! But that is not something we want to do every day. Before using my plan I was infamous for having peanut butter, no jelly. Deli meat, but no bread. Hot dogs, but no buns. You get the idea…It's kind of a running joke in our house.

My hope for this book is that it will help alleviate some of your meal planning stress. As well as equip you to be able to prepare home-cooked meals for your crew.

And since we're talking about getting rid of some stress, don't be afraid to solicit some help! Our kids are always part of the cooking process here. Whether they're helping me to prepare, doing the actual cooking, or cleaning up afterwards, we work as a team! It's great practice for them, and I've found they're all quite willing and excited to participate in the meals and planning for our family.

So make use of your resources, grab some helpers, head to the grocery store and get your meal plan on!

MONTHLY MEAL PLANS

Meal Plan for: January

Use Shopping List A

Breakfast, Lunch, Snack, Dinner

Sun	Mon	Tue	Wed	Thu	Fri	Sat
Penne Pasta Bake, Bread, Salad	Milk, Muffins & Fruit Chicken Nuggets, Fruit, Nuts Grapes, Cheese chunks, Crackers Pork Tenderloin, Baked Potatoes, Salad	Smoothies, Pancakes Pizza Bites (French bread, pizza sauce, cheese, toppings) Frozen Gogurt Taco Salad or Enchilada Casserole, Rice, Beans	Smoothies, French Toast, Sausage Fish Sticks, veggies w/ ranch Apples & Peanut Butter Corn & Cheese Chowder	Yogurt, Fruit, Granola Hot Dogs, Fruit, Chips Homemade Granola Bars Spiral Ham, Scallop Potatoes, Salad or veggie	Smoothies, Egg, ham, & cheese Bagels Grilled Sandwiches: pesto, turkey, tomato, black olives, feta cheese Veggies & Ranch Dip Mongolian Beef & Broccoli, Rice	BBQ Pulled Chicken Corn, Salad
Spaghetti, Meatballs, Salad, Bread	Smoothies, pancakes Grilled Cheese, Tomato Soup, Fruit White Chocolate Popcorn Breaded Chicken, parsley potatoes, Peas	Smoothies, Eggs, Toast Chicken Salad, Fruit (Or Cream cheese & Cucumber Sandwich) Soft Pretzels Grilled Chicken Quesadillas, Lettuce, tomato, guacamole, shredded cheese	Smoothies, French Toast Mac-n-Cheese, veggies w/ ranch Parfait (layered yogurt, fruit, granola) Pork Roast, Sweet Potatoes, Green Beans	Cottage Cheese & Fruit Bologna Sandwich Pretzels, fruit Hot Chocolate, marshmallows and graham crackers BBQ Ribs, Corn, Mashed Potatoes	Egg, ham, cheese Bagels PB & Honey w/ banana sandwich, Fruit, Pretzels Sliced cheese, meat, crackers Homemade Pizza & Salad (or order for delivery)	BBQ sauce on Polska-Kielbasa Sausage, Potatoes, Broccoli
Ravioli or Rigatoni, Meatballs, Bread, Salad	Milk, Muffins, Fruit Grilled Ham, Cheese & Tomato, Fruit Sliced Apples with Peanut Butter Pork Chops, Breaded Cauliflower, Salad	Smoothies, Pancakes Hamburgers Chips, Pickle Fruit Salsa & Tortilla Chips Creamy Chicken Burritos, guacamole, sour cream, tomatoes, lettuce etc.	Smoothies, French Toast, Sausage Mini Pizzas (French bread, pizza sauce, cheese, pepperoni) Cheese cubes w/ Pretzel toothpicks Crockpot Rotisserie Chicken, Potatoes, Veggie	Yogurt, Fruit, Granola Ham & Cream Cheese Tortilla Pinwheels, Snap Peas or Edamame Veggies & Ranch Dip Meatloaf, Mashed Potatoes, Salad or Veggie	Smoothies, Egg, ham, cheese scramble Egg Salad Sandwiches Pretzels, Pickle Diced Orange, Apple, Craisin & Walnut Salad Green Chili and Homemade Tortillas	Chicken Stir fry, Rice
Stuffed Shells, Salad, Bread	Smoothies, Eggs, Toast Tuna Salad Sandwich, Fruit, Cheese Stick Cheese and Crackers Italian Beef Pot Roast & Veggies	Smoothies, Pancakes Munchie Platter: Diced Cheese, Salami, Crackers, Fruit, veggies Chex Mix Beef, Chicken Fajitas Rice, Beans	Smoothies, French Toast Mac-n-Cheese, veggies w/ ranch PB, Honey & Banana Tortilla Pinwheels Breaded Pork Chops, Parsley Potatoes, Peas	Cottage Cheese & Fruit Salami & Provolone Sandwich, Fruit, Pretzels Carrot Sticks Tortellini Soup, Bread	Smoothies, Egg, ham, cheese Bagels Grilled Turkey, avocado, feta, sun dried tomato Panini, Pickle, Chips Veggies & Ranch Dip Coconut Chicken, potatoes, veggies	Grilled Chicken Cesar Panini's Pickle Chips
Chicken Parmesan Breaded Chicken over pasta with marinara sauce, Salad, Bread Sticks	Egg, Sausage, Cheese Burrito & Fruit Turkey & Avocado Tortilla Wraps, Fruit String Cheese and fruit Beef Brisket, Mashed Potatoes, Corn or Peas	Smoothies, pancakes Sandwich, Pasta Salad, Fruit Parfait (layered yogurt, fruit, granola) Enchiladas or Beef Burritos, Rice, Beans, lettuce etc.	Smoothies, French Toast, Sausage Fish Sticks, veggies w/ ranch Sliced cheese, meat, crackers Hot Taco Soup	Yogurt, Fruit, Granola Bologna Sandwich, fruit, pretzels Frozen Gogurt Homemade Calzones, Salad, Bread	Smoothies, Egg, ham, cheese scramble PB&J, fruit Trail Mix Breaded Chicken, baked potato, salad	Sloppy Joe's, Salad or Veggie

Meal Plan for: February

Use Shopping List A

Breakfast, Lunch, Snack, Dinner

Sun	Mon	Tue	Wed	Thu	Fri	Sat
Penne Pasta Bake, Bread, Salad	Milk, Muffins & Fruit Chicken Nuggets, Fruit, Nuts Grapes, Cheese chunks, Crackers Pork Tenderloin, Baked Potatoes, Salad	Smoothies, Pancakes Pizza Bites (French bread, pizza sauce, cheese, toppings) Frozen Gogurt Taco Salad or Enchilada Casserole, Rice, Beans	Smoothies, French Toast, Sausage Fish Sticks, veggies w/ ranch Apples & Peanut Butter Corn & Cheese Chowder	Yogurt, Fruit, Granola Hot Dogs, Fruit, Chips Homemade Granola Bars Spiral Ham, Scallop Potatoes, Salad or veggie	Smoothies, Egg, ham, & cheese Bagels Grilled Sandwiches: pesto, turkey, tomato, black olives, feta cheese Veggies & Ranch Dip Mongolian Beef & Broccoli, Rice	BBQ Pulled Chicken Corn, Salad
Spaghetti, Meatballs, Salad, Bread	Smoothies, pancakes Grilled Cheese, Tomato Soup, Fruit White Chocolate Popcorn Breaded Chicken, parsley potatoes, Peas	Smoothies, Eggs, Toast Chicken Salad, Fruit (Or Cream cheese & Cucumber Sandwich) Soft Pretzels Grilled Chicken Quesadillas, Lettuce, tomato, guacamole, shredded cheese	Smoothies, French Toast Mac-n-Cheese, veggies w/ ranch Parfait (layered yogurt, fruit, granola) Pork Roast, Sweet Potatoes, Green Beans	Cottage Cheese & Fruit Bologna Sandwich Pretzels, fruit Hot Chocolate, marshmallows and graham crackers BBQ Ribs, Corn, Mashed Potatoes	Egg, ham, cheese Bagels PB & Honey w/ banana sandwich, Fruit, Pretzels Sliced cheese, meat, crackers Homemade Pizza & Salad (or order for delivery)	BBQ sauce or Polska-Kielbasa Sausage Potatoes Broccoli
Ravioli or Rigatoni, Meatballs, Bread, Salad	Milk, Muffins, Fruit Grilled Ham, Cheese & Tomato, Fruit Sliced Apples with Peanut Butter Pork Chops, Breaded Cauliflower, Salad	Smoothies, Pancakes Hamburgers Chips, Pickle Fruit Salsa & Tortilla Chips Creamy Chicken Burritos, guacamole, sour cream, tomatoes, lettuce etc.	Smoothies, French Toast, Sausage Mini Pizzas (French bread, pizza sauce, cheese, pepperoni) Cheese cubes w/ Pretzel toothpicks Crockpot Rotisserie Chicken, Potatoes, Veggie	Yogurt, Fruit, Granola Ham & Cream Cheese Tortilla Pinwheels, Snap Peas or Edamame Veggies & Ranch Dip Meatloaf, Mashed Potatoes, Salad or Veggie	Smoothies, Egg, ham, cheese scramble Egg Salad Sandwiches Pretzels, Pickle Diced Orange, Apple, Craisin & Walnut Salad Green Chili and Homemade Tortillas	Chicken Stir fry, Rice
Stuffed Shells, Salad, Bread	Smoothies, Eggs, Toast Tuna Salad Sandwich, Fruit, Cheese Stick Cheese and Crackers Italian Beef Pot Roast & Veggies	Smoothies, Pancakes Munchie Platter: Diced Cheese, Salami, Crackers, Fruit, veggies Chex Mix Beef, Chicken Fajitas Rice, Beans	Smoothies, French Toast Mac-n-Cheese, veggies w/ ranch PB, Honey & Banana Tortilla Pinwheels Breaded Pork Chops, Parsley Potatoes, Peas	Cottage Cheese & Fruit Salami & Provolone Sandwich, Fruit, Pretzels Carrot Sticks Tortellini Soup, Bread	Smoothies, Egg, ham, cheese Bagels Grilled Turkey, avocado, feta, sun dried tomato Panini, Pickle, Chips Veggies & Ranch Dip Coconut Chicken, potatoes, veggies	Grilled Chicken Cesar Panini's Pickle Chips
Chicken Parmesan (Breaded Chicken over pasta with marinara sauce), Salad, Bread Sticks	Egg, Sausage, Cheese Burrito & Fruit Turkey & Avocado Tortilla Wraps, Fruit String Cheese and fruit Beef Brisket, Mashed Potatoes, Corn or Peas	Smoothies, pancakes Sandwich, Pasta Salad, Fruit Parfait (layered yogurt, fruit, granola) Enchiladas or Beef Burritos, Rice, Beans, lettuce etc.	Smoothies, French Toast, Sausage Fish Sticks, veggies w/ ranch Sliced cheese, meat, crackers Hot Taco Soup	Yogurt, Fruit, Granola Bologna Sandwich, fruit, pretzels Frozen Gogurt Homemade Calzones, Salad, Bread	Smoothies, Egg, ham, cheese scramble PB&J, fruit Trail Mix Breaded Chicken, baked potato, salad	Sloppy Joe's, Salad o Veggie

Meal Plan for: March

Use Shopping List A

Breakfast, Lunch, Snack, Dinner

Sun	Mon	Tue	Wed	Thu	Fri	Sat
Penne Pasta Bake, Bread, Salad	Milk, Muffins & Fruit Chicken Nuggets, Fruit, Nuts Grapes, Cheese chunks, Crackers Pork Tenderloin, Baked Potatoes, Salad	Smoothies, Pancakes Pizza Bites (French bread, pizza sauce, cheese, toppings) Frozen Gogurt Taco Salad or Enchilada Casserole, Rice, Beans	Smoothies, French Toast, Sausage Fish Sticks, veggies w/ ranch Apples & Peanut Butter Corn & Cheese Chowder	Yogurt, Fruit, Granola Hot Dogs, Fruit, Chips Homemade Granola Bars Spiral Ham, Scallop Potatoes, Salad or veggie	Smoothies, Egg, ham, & cheese Bagels Grilled Sandwiches: pesto, turkey, tomato, black olives, feta cheese Veggies & Ranch Dip Mongolian Beef & Broccoli, Rice	BBQ Pulled Chicken Corn, Salad
Spaghetti, Meatballs, Salad, Bread	Smoothies, pancakes Grilled Cheese, Tomato Soup, Fruit White Chocolate Popcorn Breaded Chicken, parsley potatoes, Peas	Smoothies, Eggs, Toast Chicken Salad, Fruit (Or Cream cheese & Cucumber Sandwich) Soft Pretzels Grilled Chicken Quesadillas, Lettuce, tomato, guacamole, shredded cheese	Smoothies, French Toast Mac-n-Cheese, veggies w/ ranch Parfait (layered yogurt, fruit, granola) Pork Roast, Sweet Potatoes, Green Beans	Cottage Cheese & Fruit Bologna Sandwich Pretzels, fruit Hot Chocolate, marshmallows and graham crackers BBQ Ribs, Corn, Mashed Potatoes	Egg, ham, cheese Bagels PB & Honey w/ banana sandwich, Fruit, Pretzels Sliced cheese, meat, crackers Homemade Pizza & Salad (or order for delivery)	BBQ sauce on Polska-Kielbasa Sausage, Potatoes, Broccoli
Ravioli or Rigatoni, Meatballs, Bread, Salad	Milk, Muffins, Fruit Grilled Ham, Cheese & Tomato, Fruit Sliced Apples with Peanut Butter Pork Chops, Breaded Cauliflower, Salad	Smoothies, Pancakes Hamburgers Chips, Pickle Fruit Salsa & Tortilla Chips Creamy Chicken Burritos, guacamole, sour cream, tomatoes, lettuce etc.	Smoothies, French Toast, Sausage Mini Pizzas(French bread, pizza sauce, cheese, pepperoni) Cheese cubes w/ Pretzel toothpicks Crockpot Rotisserie Chicken, Potatoes, Veggie	Yogurt, Fruit, Granola Ham & Cream Cheese Tortilla Pinwheels, Snap Peas or Edamame Veggies & Ranch Dip Meatloaf, Mashed Potatoes, Salad or Veggie	Smoothies, Egg, ham, cheese scramble Egg Salad Sandwiches Pretzels, Pickle Diced Orange, Apple, Craisin & Walnut Salad Green Chili and Homemade Tortillas	Chicken Stir fry, Rice
Stuffed Shells, Salad, Bread	Smoothies, Eggs, Toast Tuna Salad Sandwich, Fruit, Cheese Stick Cheese and Crackers Italian Beef Pot Roast & Veggies	Smoothies, Pancakes Munchie Platter: Diced Cheese, Salami, Crackers, Fruit, veggies Chex Mix Beef, Chicken Fajitas Rice, Beans	Smoothies, French Toast Mac-n-Cheese, veggies w/ ranch PB, Honey & Banana Tortilla Pinwheels Breaded Pork Chops, Parsley Potatoes, Peas	Cottage Cheese & Fruit Salami & Provolone Sandwich, Fruit, Pretzels Carrot Sticks Tortellini Soup, Bread	Smoothies, Egg, ham, cheese Bagels Grilled Turkey, avocado, feta, sun dried tomato Panini, Pickle, Chips Veggies & Ranch Dip Coconut Chicken, potatoes, veggies	Grilled Chicken Cesar Panini's Pickle Chips
Chicken Parmesan Breaded Chicken over pasta with marinara sauce), Salad, Bread sticks	Egg, Sausage, Cheese Burrito & Fruit Turkey & Avocado Tortilla Wraps, Fruit, String Cheese and fruit Beef Brisket, Mashed Potatoes, Corn or Peas	Smoothies, pancakes Sandwich, Pasta Salad, Fruit Parfait (layered yogurt, fruit, granola) Enchiladas or Beef Burritos, Rice, Beans, lettuce etc.	Smoothies, French Toast, Sausage Fish Sticks, veggies w/ ranch Sliced cheese, meat, crackers Hot Taco Soup	Yogurt, Fruit, Granola Bologna Sandwich, fruit, pretzels Frozen Gogurt Homemade Calzones, Salad, Bread	Smoothies, Egg, ham, cheese scramble PB&J, fruit Trail Mix Breaded Chicken, baked potato, salad	Sloppy Joe's, Salad or Veggie

Meal Plan for: April

Use Shopping List A | Breakfast, Lunch, Snack, Dinner

Sun	Mon	Tue	Wed	Thu	Fri	Sat
Penne Pasta Bake, Bread, Salad	Milk, Muffins & Fruit Chicken Nuggets, Fruit, Nuts Grapes, Cheese chunks, Crackers Pork Tenderloin, Baked Potatoes, Salad	Smoothies, Pancakes Pizza Bites (French bread, pizza sauce, cheese, toppings) Frozen Gogurt Taco Salad or Enchilada Casserole, Rice, Beans	Smoothies, French Toast, Sausage Fish Sticks, veggies w/ ranch Apples & Peanut Butter Corn & Cheese Chowder	Yogurt, Fruit, Granola Hot Dogs, Fruit, Chips Homemade Granola Bars Spiral Ham, Scallop Potatoes, Salad or veggie	Smoothies, Egg, ham, & cheese Bagels Grilled Sandwiches: pesto, turkey, tomato, black olives, feta cheese Veggies & Ranch Dip Mongolian Beef & Broccoli, Rice	BBQ Pulled Chicken Corn, Salad
Spaghetti, Meatballs, Salad, Bread	Smoothies, pancakes Grilled Cheese, Tomato Soup, Fruit White Chocolate Popcorn Breaded Chicken, parsley potatoes, Peas	Smoothies, Eggs, Toast Chicken Salad, Fruit (Or Cream cheese & Cucumber Sandwich) Soft Pretzels Grilled Chicken Quesadillas, Lettuce, tomato, guacamole, shredded cheese	Smoothies, French Toast Mac-n-Cheese, veggies w/ ranch Parfait (layered yogurt, fruit, granola) Pork Roast, Sweet Potatoes, Green Beans	Cottage Cheese & Fruit Bologna Sandwich Pretzels, fruit Hot Chocolate, marshmallows and graham crackers BBQ Ribs, Corn, Mashed Potatoes	Egg, ham, cheese Bagels PB & Honey w/ banana sandwich, Fruit, Pretzels Sliced cheese, meat, crackers Homemade Pizza & Salad (or order for delivery)	BBQ sauce or Polska-Kielbasa Sausage Potatoes Broccoli
Ravioli or Rigatoni, Meatballs, Bread, Salad	Milk, Muffins, Fruit Grilled Ham, Cheese & Tomato, Fruit Sliced Apples with Peanut Butter Pork Chops, Breaded Cauliflower, Salad	Smoothies, Pancakes Hamburgers Chips. Pickle Fruit Salsa & Tortilla Chips Creamy Chicken Burritos, guacamole, sour cream, tomatoes, lettuce etc.	Smoothies, French Toast, Sausage Mini Pizzas (French bread, pizza sauce, cheese, pepperoni) Cheese cubes w/ Pretzel toothpicks Crockpot Rotisserie Chicken, Potatoes, Veggie	Yogurt, Fruit, Granola Ham & Cream Cheese Tortilla Pinwheels, Snap Peas or Edamame Veggies & Ranch Dip Meatloaf, Mashed Potatoes, Salad or Veggie	Smoothies, Egg, ham, cheese scramble Egg Salad Sandwiches Pretzels, Pickle Diced Orange, Apple, Craisin & Walnut Salad Green Chili and Homemade Tortillas	Chicken Stir fry, Rice
Stuffed Shells, Salad, Bread	Smoothies, Eggs, Toast Tuna Salad Sandwich, Fruit, Cheese Stick Cheese and Crackers Italian Beef Pot Roast & Veggies	Smoothies, Pancakes Munchie Platter: Diced Cheese, Salami, Crackers, Fruit, veggies Chex Mix Beef, Chicken Fajitas Rice, Beans	Smoothies, French Toast Mac-n-Cheese, veggies w/ ranch PB, Honey & Banana Tortilla Pinwheels Breaded Pork Chops, Parsley Potatoes, Peas	Cottage Cheese & Fruit Salami & Provolone Sandwich, Fruit, Pretzels Carrot Sticks Tortellini Soup, Bread	Smoothies, Egg, ham, cheese Bagels Grilled Turkey, avocado, feta, sun dried tomato Panini, Pickle, Chips Veggies & Ranch Dip Coconut Chicken, potatoes, veggies	Grilled Chicken Cesar Panini's Pickle Chips
Chicken Parmesan (Breaded Chicken over pasta with marinara sauce), Salad, Bread Sticks	Egg, Sausage, Cheese Burrito & Fruit Turkey & Avocado Tortilla Wraps, Fruit String Cheese and fruit Beef Brisket, Mashed Potatoes, Corn or Peas	Smoothies, pancakes Sandwich, Pasta Salad, Fruit Parfait (layered yogurt, fruit, granola) Enchiladas or Beef Burritos, Rice, Beans, lettuce etc.	Smoothies, French Toast, Sausage Fish Sticks, veggies w/ ranch Sliced cheese, meat, crackers Hot Taco Soup	Yogurt, Fruit, Granola Bologna Sandwich, fruit, pretzels Frozen Gogurt Homemade Calzones, Salad, Bread	Smoothies, Egg, ham, cheese scramble PB&J, fruit Trail Mix Breaded Chicken, baked potato, salad	Sloppy Joe's, Salad or Veggie

Meal Plan for: May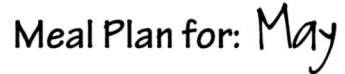

Use Shopping List B   Breakfast, Lunch, Snack, Dinner

Sun	Mon	Tue	Wed	Thu	Fri	Sat
Penne Pasta Bake, Bread, Salad	Milk, Muffins & Fruit / Chicken Nuggets, Fruit, Nuts / Grapes, Cheese chunks, Crackers / Pork Tenderloin, Baked Potatoes, Salad	Smoothies, Pancakes / Pizza Bites (French bread, pizza sauce, cheese, toppings) / Frozen Gogurt / Taco Salad or Enchilada Casserole, Rice, Beans	Smoothies, French Toast, Sausage / Fish Sticks, veggies w. ranch / Apples & Peanut Butter / Beef Stroganoff, Broccoli	Yogurt, Fruit, Granola / Hot Dogs, Fruit, Chips / Homemade Granola Bars / Spiral Ham, Scallop Potatoes, Salad or Veggie	Smoothies, Egg, ham, cheese Bagels / Grilled Sandwiches: pesto, turkey, tomato, black olives, feta cheese / Veggies & Ranch Dip / Mongolian Beef & Broccoli, Rice	BBQ Pulled Chicken, Corn, Salad
Spaghetti, Meatballs, Salad, Bread	Smoothies, Eggs, Toast / Grilled Cheese, Tomato Soup Fruit / Popcorn / Breaded Chicken, parsley potatoes, Peas	Smoothies, Pancakes / Chicken Salad, Fruit (Or Cream cheese & Cucumber Sandwich) / Soft Pretzels / Beef Burritos, Rice	Smoothies, French Toast / Mac-n-Cheese, veggies w. ranch / Parfait (layered yogurt, fruit, granola) / Pork Roast, Sweet Potatoes, Green Beans	Cottage Cheese & Fruit / Bologna Sandwich Pretzels, fruit / Graham Crackers, Cream Cheese, Jelly / BBQ Ribs, Corn, Mashed Potatoes	Egg, ham, cheese scramble / PB & Honey w. Fruit, Pretzels / Sliced cheese, meat, crackers / BBQ Pork Sandwiches (Use leftover Pork from Wed) Pork-n-beans, Corn	Grill: Steak, Veggie Kabobs: onion, mushroom tomato, green peppers, Pasta Salad
Ravioli, Meatballs, Bread, Salad	Milk, Muffins, Fruit / Grilled Ham & Cheese, Fruit / Sliced Apples with Peanut Butter / Pork Chops, Breaded Cauliflower, Salad	Smoothies, Pancakes / Hamburgers Chips, Pickle / Fruit Salsa / Creamy Chicken Burritos, guacamole, sour cream, tomatoes, lettuce	Smoothies, French Toast, Sausage / Mini Pizzas(French bread, pizza sauce, cheese, pepperoni) / Cheese cubes w. Pretzel toothpicks / Chicken Lettuce Wraps, Fried Rice	Yogurt, Fruit, Granola / Ham & Cream Cheese Tortilla Pinwheels, Snap Peas or Edamame / Veggies & Ranch Dip / Homemade Calzones, Salad	Smoothies, Egg, ham, cheese scramble / Egg Salad Sandwiches Pretzels, Pickle / Diced Orange, Apple, Craisin & Walnut Salad / French Dip Sandwich, Potatoes, Salad	Grill: Chicken Shish-Ka-Bobs, Corn on Cob, Pasta Salad
Stuffed Shells, Salad, Bread	Smoothies, Eggs, Toast / Tuna Salad Sandwich, Fruit, Cheese Sticks / Cheese and Crackers / Italian Beef Pot Roast & Veggies	Smoothies, Pancakes / Munchie Platter: Diced Cheese, Salami, Crackers, Fruit, veggies / Chex Mix / Beef, Chicken Fajitas, Rice, Beans	Smoothies, French Toast / Mac-n-Cheese, Veggies w. ranch / Fresh Fruit Salad, nuts / Sweet-n-Sour Pork Chops, Parsley Potatoes, Peas	Cottage Cheese & Fruit / Salami & Provolone Sandwich, Fruit, Pretzels / Carrot Sticks / Tortellini Soup, Bread	Smoothies, Egg, ham, cheese Bagels / Grilled Turkey, avocado, feta, sun dried tomato Panini, Pickle, Chips / Veggies & Ranch Dip / Coconut Chicken, potatoes, veggies	Grill: Hamburgers lettuce, tomato, cheese, Potato Salad or Chips
Chicken Parmesan Breaded Chicken over pasta with marinara sauce), Salad, Bread sticks	Egg, Sausage, Cheese Burrito & Fruit / Turkey & Avocado Tortilla Wraps & Fruit / String Cheese and fruit / Beef Brisket, Mashed Potatoes, Corn or Peas	Smoothies, Pancakes / Sandwich, Pasta Salad, Fruit / Parfait (layered yogurt, fruit, granola) / Enchiladas or Beef Burritos, Rice, Beans, lettuce etc.	Smoothies, French Toast, Sausage / Fish Sticks, veggies w. ranch / Sliced cheese, meat, crackers / Breaded Chicken, Pasta Salad	Yogurt, Fruit, Granola / Bologna Sandwich, fruit, pretzels / Frozen Gogurt / Tater-Tot Casserole & Veggies	Smoothies, Egg, ham, cheese scramble / PB&J, fruit Trail Mix / BBQ Brats or Hog Dogs, Pasta Salad, Watermelon	Sloppy Joe's, Salad or veggie

Meal Plan for: June

Use Shopping List B

Breakfast, Lunch, Snack, Dinner

Sun	Mon	Tue	Wed	Thu	Fri	Sat
Penne Pasta Bake, Bread, Salad	Milk, Muffins & Fruit / Chicken Nuggets, Fruit, Nuts / Grapes, Cheese chunks, Crackers / Pork Tenderloin, Baked Potatoes, Salad	Smoothies, Pancakes / Pizza Bites (French bread, pizza sauce, cheese, toppings) / Frozen Gogurt / Taco Salad or Enchilada Casserole, Rice, Beans	Smoothies, French Toast, Sausage / Fish Sticks, veggies w/ ranch / Apples & Peanut Butter / Beef Stroganoff, Broccoli	Yogurt, Fruit, Granola / Hot Dogs, Fruit, Chips / Homemade Granola Bars / Spiral Ham, Scallop Potatoes, Salad or Veggie	Smoothies, Egg, ham, cheese Bagels / Grilled Sandwiches: pesto, turkey, tomato, black olives, feta cheese / Veggies & Ranch Dip / Mongolian Beef & Broccoli, Rice	BBQ Pulled Chicken, Corn, Salad
Spaghetti, Meatballs, Salad, Bread	Smoothies, Eggs, Toast / Grilled Cheese, Tomato Soup Fruit / Popcorn / Breaded Chicken, parsley potatoes, Peas	Smoothies, Pancakes / Chicken Salad, Fruit (Or Cream cheese & Cucumber Sandwich) / Soft Pretzels / Beef Burritos, Rice	Smoothies, French Toast / Mac-n-Cheese, veggies w/ ranch / Parfait (layered yogurt, fruit, granola) / Pork Roast, Sweet Potatoes, Green Beans	Cottage Cheese & Fruit / Bologna Sandwich Pretzels, fruit / Graham Crackers, Cream Cheese, Jelly / BBQ Ribs, Corn, Mashed Potatoes	Egg, ham, cheese scramble / PB & Honey w/ Fruit, Pretzels / Sliced cheese, meat, crackers / BBQ Pork Sandwiches (Use leftover Pork from Wed) Pork-n-beans, Corn	Grill: Steak, Veggie Kabobs: onion, mushroom, tomato, green peppers, Pasta Salad
Ravioli, Meatballs, Bread, Salad	Milk, Muffins, Fruit / Grilled Ham & Cheese, Fruit / Sliced Apples with Peanut Butter / Pork Chops, Breaded Cauliflower, Salad	Smoothies, Pancakes / Hamburgers Chips, Pickle / Fruit Salsa / Creamy Chicken Burritos, guacamole, sour cream, tomatoes, lettuce	Smoothies, French Toast, Sausage / Mini Pizzas (French bread, pizza sauce, cheese, pepperoni) / Cheese cubes w/ Pretzel toothpicks / Chicken Lettuce Wraps, Fried Rice	Yogurt, Fruit, Granola / Ham & Cream Cheese Tortilla Pinwheels, Snap Peas or Edamame / Veggies & Ranch Dip / Homemade Calzones, Salad	Smoothies, Egg, ham, cheese scramble / Egg Salad Sandwiches Pretzels, Pickle / Diced Orange, Apple, Craisin & Walnut Salad / French Dip Sandwich, Potatoes, Salad	Grill: Chicken Shish-Ka Bobs, Corn on Cob, Pasta Salad
Stuffed Shells, Salad, Bread	Smoothies, Eggs, Toast / Tuna Salad Sandwich, Fruit, Cheese Sticks / Cheese and Crackers / Italian Beef Pot Roast & Veggies	Smoothies, Pancakes / Munchie Platter: Diced Cheese, Salami, Crackers, Fruit, veggies Chex Mix / Beef, Chicken Fajitas, Rice, Beans	Smoothies, French Toast / Mac-n-Cheese, Veggies w/ ranch / Fresh Fruit Salad, nuts / Sweet-n-Sour Pork Chops, Parsley Potatoes, Peas	Cottage Cheese & Fruit / Salami & Provolone Sandwich, Fruit, Pretzels / Carrot Sticks / Tortellini Soup, Bread	Smoothies, Egg, ham, cheese Bagels / Grilled Turkey, avocado, feta, sun dried tomato Panini, Pickle, Chips / Veggies & Ranch Dip / Coconut Chicken, potatoes, veggies	Grill: Hamburger lettuce, tomato, cheese, Potato Salad or Chips
Chicken Parmesan (Breaded Chicken over pasta with marinara sauce), Salad, Bread Sticks	Egg, Sausage, Cheese Burrito & Fruit / Turkey & Avocado Tortilla Wraps & Fruit / String Cheese and fruit / Beef Brisket, Mashed Potatoes, Corn or Peas	Smoothies, Pancakes / Sandwich, Pasta Salad, Fruit / Parfait (layered yogurt, fruit, granola) / Enchiladas or Beef Burritos, Rice, Beans, lettuce etc.	Smoothies, French Toast, Sausage / Fish Sticks, veggies w/ ranch / Sliced cheese, meat, crackers / Breaded Chicken, Pasta Salad	Yogurt, Fruit, Granola / Bologna Sandwich, fruit, pretzels / Frozen Gogurt / Tater-Tot Casserole & Veggies	Smoothies, Egg, ham, cheese scramble / PB&J, fruit / Trail Mix / BBQ Brats or Hog Dogs, Pasta Salad, Watermelon	Sloppy Joe's, Salad or veggie

Meal Plan for: July

Use Shopping List B

Breakfast, Lunch, Snack, Dinner

Sun	Mon	Tue	Wed	Thu	Fri	Sat
Penne Pasta Bake, Bread, Salad	Milk, Muffins & Fruit Chicken Nuggets, Fruit, Nuts Grapes, Cheese chunks, Crackers Pork Tenderloin, Baked Potatoes, Salad	Smoothies, Pancakes Pizza Bites (French bread, pizza sauce, cheese, toppings) Frozen Gogurt Taco Salad or Enchilada Casserole, Rice, Beans	Smoothies, French Toast, Sausage Fish Sticks, veggies w/ ranch Apples & Peanut Butter Beef Stroganoff, Broccoli	Yogurt, Fruit, Granola Hot Dogs, Fruit, Chips Homemade Granola Bars Spiral Ham, Scallop Potatoes, Salad or Veggie	Smoothies, Egg, ham, cheese Bagels Grilled Sandwiches: pesto, turkey, tomato, black olives, feta cheese Veggies & Ranch Dip Mongolian Beef & Broccoli, Rice	BBQ Pulled Chicken, Corn, Salad
Spaghetti, Meatballs, Salad, Bread	Smoothies, Eggs, Toast Grilled Cheese, Tomato Soup Fruit Popcorn Breaded Chicken, parsley potatoes, Peas	Smoothies, Pancakes Chicken Salad, Fruit (Or Cream cheese & Cucumber Sandwich) Soft Pretzels Beef Burritos, Rice	Smoothies, French Toast Mac-n-Cheese, veggies w/ ranch Parfait (layered yogurt, fruit, granola) Pork Roast, Sweet Potatoes, Green Beans	Cottage Cheese & Fruit Bologna Sandwich Pretzels, fruit Graham Crackers, Cream Cheese, Jelly BBQ Ribs, Corn, Mashed Potatoes	Egg, ham, cheese scramble PB & Honey w/ Fruit, Pretzels Sliced cheese, meat, crackers BBQ Pork Sandwiches (Use leftover Pork from Wed) Pork-n-beans, Corn	Grill: Steak, Veggie Kabobs: onion, mushroom tomato, green peppers, Pasta Salad
Ravioli, Meatballs, Bread, Salad	Milk, Muffins, Fruit Grilled Ham & Cheese, Fruit Sliced Apples with Peanut Butter Pork Chops, Breaded Cauliflower, Salad	Smoothies, Pancakes Hamburgers Chips, Pickle Fruit Salsa Creamy Chicken Burritos, guacamole, sour cream, tomatoes, lettuce	Smoothies, French Toast, Sausage Mini Pizzas (French bread, pizza sauce, cheese, pepperoni) Cheese cubes w/ Pretzel toothpicks Chicken Lettuce Wraps, Fried Rice	Yogurt, Fruit, Granola Ham & Cream Cheese Tortilla Pinwheels, Snap Peas or Edamame Veggies & Ranch Dip Homemade Calzones, Salad	Smoothies, Egg, ham, cheese scramble Egg Salad Sandwiches Pretzels, Pickle Diced Orange, Apple, Craisin & Walnut Salad French Dip Sandwich, Potatoes, Salad	Grill: Chicken Shish-Ka-Bobs, Corn on Cob, Pasta Salad
Stuffed Shells, Salad, Bread	Smoothies, Eggs, Toast Tuna Salad Sandwich, Fruit, Cheese Sticks Cheese and Crackers Italian Beef Pot Roast & Veggies	Smoothies, Pancakes Munchie Platter: Diced Cheese, Salami, Crackers, Fruit, veggies Chex Mix Beef, Chicken Fajitas, Rice, Beans	Smoothies, French Toast Mac-n-Cheese, Veggies w/ ranch Fresh Fruit Salad, nuts Sweet-n-Sour Pork Chops, Parsley Potatoes, Peas	Cottage Cheese & Fruit Salami & Provolone Sandwich, Fruit, Pretzels Carrot Sticks Tortellini Soup, Bread	Smoothies, Egg, ham, cheese Bagels Grilled Turkey, avocado, feta, sun dried tomato Panini, Pickle, Chips Veggies & Ranch Dip Coconut Chicken, potatoes, veggies	Grill: Hamburgers lettuce, tomato, cheese, Potato Salad or Chips
Chicken Parmesan Breaded Chicken over pasta with marinara sauce), Salad, Bread sticks	Egg, Sausage, Cheese Burrito & Fruit Turkey & Avocado Tortilla Wraps & Fruit String Cheese and fruit Beef Brisket, Mashed Potatoes, Corn or Peas	Smoothies, Pancakes Sandwich, Pasta Salad, Fruit Parfait (layered yogurt, fruit, granola) Enchiladas or Beef Burritos, Rice, Beans, lettuce etc.	Smoothies, French Toast, Sausage Fish Sticks, veggies w/ ranch Sliced cheese, meat, crackers Breaded Chicken, Pasta Salad	Yogurt, Fruit, Granola Bologna Sandwich, fruit, pretzels Frozen Gogurt Tater-Tot Casserole & Veggies	Smoothies, Egg, ham, cheese scramble PB&J, fruit Trail Mix BBQ Brats or Hog Dogs, Pasta Salad, Watermelon	Sloppy Joe's, Salad or veggie

Meal Plan for: August

Use Shopping List B

Breakfast, Lunch, Snack, Dinner

Sun	Mon	Tue	Wed	Thu	Fri	Sat
Penne Pasta Bake, Bread, Salad	Milk, Muffins & Fruit / Chicken Nuggets, Fruit, Nuts / Grapes, Cheese chunks, Crackers / Pork Tenderloin, Baked Potatoes, Salad	Smoothies, Pancakes / Pizza Bites (French bread, pizza sauce, cheese, toppings) / Frozen Gogurt / Taco Salad or Enchilada Casserole, Rice, Beans	Smoothies, French Toast, Sausage / Fish Sticks, veggies w/ ranch / Apples & Peanut Butter / Beef Stroganoff, Broccoli	Yogurt, Fruit, Granola / Hot Dogs, Fruit, Chips / Homemade Granola Bars / Spiral Ham, Scallop Potatoes, Salad or Veggie	Smoothies, Egg, ham, cheese Bagels / Grilled Sandwiches: pesto, turkey, tomato, black olives, feta cheese / Veggies & Ranch Dip / Mongolian Beef & Broccoli, Rice	BBQ Pulled Chicken, Corn, Salad
Spaghetti, Meatballs, Salad, Bread	Smoothies, Eggs, Toast / Grilled Cheese, Tomato Soup Fruit / Popcorn / Breaded Chicken, parsley potatoes, Peas	Smoothies, Pancakes / Chicken Salad, Fruit (Or Cream cheese & Cucumber Sandwich) / Soft Pretzels / Beef Burritos, Rice	Smoothies, French Toast / Mac-n-Cheese, veggies w/ ranch / Parfait (layered yogurt, fruit, granola) / Pork Roast, Sweet Potatoes, Green Beans	Cottage Cheese & Fruit / Bologna Sandwich Pretzels, fruit / Graham Crackers, Cream Cheese, Jelly / BBQ Ribs, Corn, Mashed Potatoes	Egg, ham, cheese scramble / PB & Honey w/ Fruit, Pretzels / Sliced cheese, meat, crackers / BBQ Pork Sandwiches (Use leftover Pork from Wed) Pork-n-beans, Corn	Grill: Steak, Veggie Kabobs: onion, mushroom, tomato, green peppers, Pasta Salad
Ravioli, Meatballs, Bread, Salad	Milk, Muffins, Fruit / Grilled Ham & Cheese, Fruit / Sliced Apples with Peanut Butter / Pork Chops, Breaded Cauliflower, Salad	Smoothies, Pancakes / Hamburgers Chips, Pickle / Fruit Salsa / Creamy Chicken Burritos, guacamole, sour cream, tomatoes, lettuce	Smoothies, French Toast, Sausage / Mini Pizzas (French bread, pizza sauce, cheese, pepperoni) / Cheese cubes w/ Pretzel toothpicks / Chicken Lettuce Wraps, Fried Rice	Yogurt, Fruit, Granola / Ham & Cream Cheese Tortilla Pinwheels, Snap Peas or Edamame / Veggies & Ranch Dip / Homemade Calzones, Salad	Smoothies, Egg, ham, cheese scramble / Egg Salad Sandwiches Pretzels, Pickle / Diced Orange, Apple, Craisin & Walnut Salad / French Dip Sandwich, Potatoes, Salad	Grill: Chicken Shish-Ka Bobs, Corn on Cob, Pasta Salad
Stuffed Shells, Salad, Bread	Smoothies, Eggs, Toast / Tuna Salad Sandwich, Fruit, Cheese Sticks / Cheese and Crackers / Italian Beef Pot Roast & Veggies	Smoothies, Pancakes / Munchie Platter: Diced Cheese, Salami, Crackers, Fruit, veggies Chex Mix / Beef, Chicken Fajitas, Rice, Beans	Smoothies, French Toast / Mac-n-Cheese, Veggies w/ ranch / Fresh Fruit Salad, nuts / Sweet-n-Sour Pork Chops, Parsley Potatoes, Peas	Cottage Cheese & Fruit / Salami & Provolone Sandwich, Fruit, Pretzels / Carrot Sticks / Tortellini Soup, Bread	Smoothies, Egg, ham, cheese Bagels / Grilled Turkey, avocado, feta, sun dried tomato Panini, Pickle, Chips / Veggies & Ranch Dip / Coconut Chicken, potatoes, veggies	Grill: Hamburger lettuce, tomato, cheese, Potato Salad or Chips
Chicken Parmesan (Breaded Chicken over pasta with marinara sauce), Salad, Bread Sticks	Egg, Sausage, Cheese Burrito & Fruit / Turkey & Avocado Tortilla Wraps & Fruit / String Cheese and fruit / Beef Brisket, Mashed Potatoes, Corn or Peas	Smoothies, Pancakes / Sandwich, Pasta Salad, Fruit / Parfait (layered yogurt, fruit, granola) / Enchiladas or Beef Burritos, Rice, Beans, lettuce etc.	Smoothies, French Toast, Sausage / Fish Sticks, veggies w/ ranch / Sliced cheese, meat, crackers / Breaded Chicken, Pasta Salad	Yogurt, Fruit, Granola / Bologna Sandwich, fruit, pretzels / Frozen Gogurt / Tater-Tot Casserole & Veggies	Smoothies, Egg, ham, cheese scramble / PB&J, fruit / Trail Mix / BBQ Brats or Hog Dogs, Pasta Salad, Watermelon	Sloppy Joe's, Salad or veggie

Meal Plan for: September

Use Shopping List B

Breakfast, Lunch, Snack, Dinner

Sun	Mon	Tue	Wed	Thu	Fri	Sat
Penne Pasta Bake, Bread, Salad	Milk, Muffins & Fruit Chicken Nuggets, Fruit, Nuts Grapes, Cheese chunks, Crackers Pork Tenderloin, Baked Potatoes, Salad	Smoothies, Pancakes Pizza Bites (French bread, pizza sauce, cheese, toppings) Frozen Gogurt Taco Salad or Enchilada Casserole, Rice, Beans	Smoothies, French Toast, Sausage Fish Sticks, veggies w/ ranch Apples & Peanut Butter Beef Stroganoff, Broccoli	Yogurt, Fruit, Granola Hot Dogs, Fruit, Chips Homemade Granola Bars Spiral Ham, Scallop Potatoes, Salad or Veggie	Smoothies, Egg, ham, cheese Bagels Grilled Sandwiches: pesto, turkey, tomato, black olives, feta cheese Veggies & Ranch Dip Mongolian Beef & Broccoli, Rice	BBQ Chicken, Corn, Salad
Spaghetti, Meatballs, Salad, Bread	Smoothies, Eggs, Toast Grilled Cheese, Tomato Soup Fruit Popcorn Breaded Chicken, parsley potatoes, Peas	Smoothies, Pancakes Chicken Salad, Fruit (Or Cream cheese & Cucumber Sandwich) Soft Pretzels Beef Burritos, Rice	Smoothies, French Toast Mac-n-Cheese, veggies w/ ranch Parfait (layered yogurt, fruit, granola) Pork Roast, Sweet Potatoes, Green Beans	Cottage Cheese & Fruit Bologna Sandwich Pretzels, fruit Graham Crackers, Cream Cheese, Jelly BBQ Ribs, Corn, Mashed Potatoes	Egg, ham, cheese scramble PB & Honey w/ Fruit, Pretzels Sliced cheese, meat, crackers BBQ Pork Sandwiches (Use leftover Pork from Wed) Pork-n-beans, Corn	Grill: Steak, Veggie Kabobs: onion, mushroom tomato, green peppers, Pasta Salad
Ravioli, Meatballs, Bread, Salad	Milk, Muffins, Fruit Grilled Ham & Cheese, Fruit Sliced Apples with Peanut Butter Pork Chops, Breaded Cauliflower, Salad	Smoothies, Pancakes Hamburgers Chips, Pickle Fruit Salsa Creamy Chicken Burritos, guacamole, sour cream, tomatoes, lettuce	Smoothies, French Toast, Sausage Mini Pizzas (French bread, pizza sauce, cheese, pepperoni) Cheese cubes w/ Pretzel toothpicks Chicken Lettuce Wraps, Fried Rice	Yogurt, Fruit, Granola Ham & Cream Cheese Tortilla Pinwheels, Snap Peas or Edamame Veggies & Ranch Dip Homemade Calzones, Salad	Smoothies, Egg, ham, cheese scramble Egg Salad Sandwiches Pretzels, Pickle Diced Orange, Apple, Craisin & Walnut Salad French Dip Sandwich, Potatoes, Salad	Grill: Chicken Shish-Ka-Bobs, Corn on Cob, Pasta Salad
Stuffed Shells, Salad, Bread	Smoothies, Eggs, Toast Tuna Salad Sandwich, Fruit, Cheese Sticks Cheese and Crackers Italian Beef Pot Roast & Veggies	Smoothies, Pancakes Munchie Platter: Diced Cheese, Salami, Crackers, Fruit, veggies Chex Mix Beef, Chicken Fajitas, Rice, Beans	Smoothies, French Toast Mac-n-Cheese, Veggies w/ ranch Fresh Fruit Salad, nuts Sweet-n-Sour Pork Chops, Parsley Potatoes, Peas	Cottage Cheese & Fruit Salami & Provolone Sandwich, Fruit, Pretzels Carrot Sticks Tortellini Soup, Bread	Smoothies, Egg, ham, cheese Bagels Grilled Turkey, avocado, feta, sun dried tomato Panini, Pickle, Chips Veggies & Ranch Dip Coconut Chicken, potatoes, veggies	Grill: Hamburgers lettuce, tomato, cheese, Potato Salad or Chips
Chicken Parmesan Breaded Chicken over pasta with marinara sauce, Salad, Bread sticks	Egg, Sausage, Cheese Burrito & Fruit Turkey & Avocado Tortilla Wraps & Fruit String Cheese and fruit Beef Brisket, Mashed Potatoes, Corn or Peas	Smoothies, Pancakes Sandwich, Pasta Salad, Fruit Parfait (layered yogurt, fruit, granola) Enchiladas or Beef Burritos, Rice, Beans, lettuce etc.	Smoothies, French Toast, Sausage Fish Sticks, veggies w/ ranch Sliced cheese, meat, crackers Breaded Chicken, Pasta Salad	Yogurt, Fruit, Granola Bologna Sandwich, fruit, pretzels Frozen Gogurt Tater-Tot Casserole & Veggies	Smoothies, Egg, ham, cheese scramble PB&J, fruit Trail Mix BBQ Brats or Hot Dogs, Pasta Salad, Watermelon	Sloppy Joe's, Salad or veggie

Meal Plan for: October

Use Shopping List C

Breakfast, Lunch, Snack, Dinner

Sun	Mon	Tue	Wed	Thu	Fri	Sat
Penne Pasta Bake, Bread, Salad	Milk, Muffins & Fruit Chicken Nuggets, Fruit, Nuts Grapes, Cheese chunks, Crackers Pork Tenderloin, Baked Potatoes, Salad	Smoothies, Pancakes Pizza Bites (French bread, pizza sauce, cheese, toppings) Frozen Gogurt Taco Salad or Enchilada Casserole, Rice, Beans	Smoothies, French Toast, Sausage Fish Sticks, veggies w/ ranch Apples & Peanut Butter Corn & Cheese Chowder	Yogurt, Fruit, Granola Hot Dogs, Fruit, Chips Homemade Granola Bars Spiral Ham, Scallop Potatoes, Salad or veggie	Smoothies, Egg, ham, & cheese Bagels Grilled Sandwiches: pesto, turkey, tomato, black olives, feta cheese Veggies & Ranch Dip Ham and white bean soup (Use leftover ham from Thur.)	BBQ Chicken Corn, Salad
Spaghetti, Meatballs, Salad, Bread	Smoothies, pancakes Grilled Cheese, Tomato Soup, Fruit White Chocolate Popcorn Breaded Chicken, parsley potatoes, Peas	Smoothies, Eggs, Toast Chicken Salad, Fruit (Or Cream cheese & Cucumber Sandwich) Soft Pretzels Grilled Chicken Quesadillas, Lettuce, tomato, guacamole, shredded cheese	Smoothies, French Toast Mac-n-Cheese, veggies w/ ranch Parfait (layered yogurt, fruit, granola) Pork Roast, Sweet Potatoes, Green Beans	Cottage Cheese & Fruit Bologna Sandwich Pretzels, fruit Hot Chocolate, marshmallows and graham crackers BBQ Ribs, Corn, Mashed Potatoes	Egg, ham, cheese Bagels PB & Honey w/ banana sandwich, Fruit, Pretzels Sliced cheese, meat, crackers Homemade Pizza & Salad (or order for delivery)	BBQ sauce on Polska-Kielbasa Sausage Potatoes Broccoli
Ravioli or Rigatoni, Meatballs, Bread, Salad	Milk, Muffins, Fruit Grilled Ham, Cheese & Tomato, Fruit Sliced Apples with Peanut Butter Pork Chops, Breaded Cauliflower, Salad	Smoothies, Pancakes Hamburgers Chips, Pickle Fruit Salsa & Tortilla Chips Creamy Chicken Burritos, guacamole, sour cream, tomatoes, lettuce etc.	Smoothies, French Toast, Sausage Mini Pizzas (French bread, pizza sauce, cheese, pepperoni) Cheese cubes w/ Pretzel toothpicks Crockpot Rotisserie Chicken, Potatoes, Veggie	Yogurt, Fruit, Granola Ham & Cream Cheese Tortilla Pinwheels, Snap Peas or Edamame Veggies & Ranch Dip Meatloaf, Mashed Potatoes, Salad or Veggie	Smoothies, Egg, ham, cheese scramble Egg Salad Sandwiches Pretzels, Pickle Diced Orange, Apple, Craisin & Walnut Salad Green Chili and Homemade Tortillas	Chicken Stir fry, Rice
Stuffed Shells, Salad, Bread	Smoothies, Eggs, Toast Tuna Salad Sandwich, Fruit, Cheese Stick Cheese and Crackers Italian Beef Pot Roast & Veggies	Smoothies, Pancakes Munchie Platter: Diced Cheese, Salami, Crackers, Fruit, veggies Chex Mix Beef, Chicken Fajitas Rice, Beans	Smoothies, French Toast Mac-n-Cheese, veggies w/ ranch PB, Honey & Banana Tortilla Pinwheels Breaded Pork Chops, Parsley Potatoes, Peas	Cottage Cheese & Fruit Salami & Provolone Sandwich, Fruit, Pretzels Carrot Sticks Tortellini Soup, Bread	Smoothies, Egg, ham, cheese Bagels Grilled Turkey, avocado, feta, sun dried tomato Panini, Pickle, Chips Veggies & Ranch Dip Coconut Chicken, potatoes, veggies	Grilled Chicken Cesar Panini, Pickle Chips
Chicken Parmesan (Breaded Chicken over pasta with marinara sauce), Salad, Bread Sticks	Egg, Sausage, Cheese Burrito & Fruit Turkey & Avocado Tortilla Wraps, Fruit String Cheese and fruit Beef Brisket, Mashed Potatoes, Corn or Peas	Smoothies, pancakes Sandwich, Pasta Salad, Fruit Parfait (layered yogurt, fruit, granola) Enchiladas or Beef Burritos, Rice, Beans, lettuce etc.	Smoothies, French Toast, Sausage Fish Sticks, veggies w/ ranch Sliced cheese, meat, crackers Hot Taco Soup	Yogurt, Fruit, Granola Bologna Sandwich, fruit, pretzels Frozen Gogurt Homemade Calzones, Salad, Bread	Smoothies, Egg, ham, cheese scramble PB&J, fruit Trail Mix Breaded Chicken, baked potato, salad	Sloppy Joe's, Salad or Veggie

Meal Plan for: November

Use Shopping List C

Breakfast, Lunch, Snack, Dinner

Sun	Mon	Tue	Wed	Thu	Fri	Sat
Penne Pasta Bake, Bread, Salad	Milk, Muffins & Fruit Chicken Nuggets, Fruit, Nuts Grapes, Cheese chunks, Crackers Pork Tenderloin, Baked Potatoes, Salad	Smoothies, Pancakes Pizza Bites (French bread, pizza sauce, cheese, toppings) Frozen Gogurt Taco Salad or Enchilada Casserole, Rice, Beans	Smoothies, French Toast, Sausage Fish Sticks, veggies w/ ranch Apples & Peanut Butter Corn & Cheese Chowder	Yogurt, Fruit, Granola Hot Dogs, Fruit, Chips Homemade Granola Bars Spiral Ham, Scallop Potatoes, Salad or veggie	Smoothies, Egg, ham, & cheese Bagels Grilled Sandwiches: pesto, turkey, tomato, black olives, feta cheese Veggies & Ranch Dip Ham and white bean soup (Use leftover ham from Thur.)	BBQ Pulled Chicken Corn, Salad
Spaghetti, Meatballs, Salad, Bread	Smoothies, pancakes Grilled Cheese, Tomato Soup, Fruit White Chocolate Popcorn Breaded Chicken, parsley potatoes, Peas	Smoothies, Eggs, Toast Chicken Salad, Fruit (Or Cream cheese & Cucumber Sandwich) Soft Pretzels Grilled Chicken Quesadillas, Lettuce, tomato, guacamole, shredded cheese	Smoothies, French Toast Mac-n-Cheese, veggies w/ ranch Parfait (layered yogurt, fruit, granola) Pork Roast, Sweet Potatoes, Green Beans	Cottage Cheese & Fruit Bologna Sandwich Pretzels, fruit Hot Chocolate, marshmallows and graham crackers BBQ Ribs, Corn, Mashed Potatoes	Egg, ham, cheese Bagels PB & Honey w/ banana sandwich, Fruit, Pretzels Sliced cheese, meat, crackers Homemade Pizza & Salad (or order for delivery)	BBQ sauce on Polska-Kielbasa Sausage, Potatoes, Broccoli
Ravioli or Rigatoni, Meatballs, Bread, Salad	Milk, Muffins, Fruit Grilled Ham, Cheese & Tomato, Fruit Sliced Apples with Peanut Butter Pork Chops, Breaded Cauliflower, Salad	Smoothies, Pancakes Hamburgers Chips, Pickle Fruit Salsa & Tortilla Chips Creamy Chicken Burritos, guacamole, sour cream, tomatoes, lettuce etc.	Smoothies, French Toast, Sausage Mini Pizzas(French bread, pizza sauce, cheese, pepperoni) Cheese cubes w/ Pretzel toothpicks Crockpot Rotisserie Chicken, Potatoes, Veggie	Yogurt, Fruit, Granola Ham & Cream Cheese Tortilla Pinwheels, Snap Peas or Edamame Veggies & Ranch Dip Meatloaf, Mashed Potatoes, Salad or Veggie	Smoothies, Egg, ham, cheese scramble Egg Salad Sandwiches Pretzels, Pickle Diced Orange, Apple, Craisin & Walnut Salad Green Chili and Homemade Tortillas	Chicken Stir fry, Rice
Stuffed Shells, Salad, Bread	Smoothies, Eggs, Toast Tuna Salad Sandwich, Fruit, Cheese Stick Cheese and Crackers Italian Beef Pot Roast & Veggies	Smoothies, Pancakes Munchie Platter: Diced Cheese, Salami, Crackers, Fruit, veggies Chex Mix Beef, Chicken Fajitas Rice, Beans	Smoothies, French Toast Mac-n-Cheese, veggies w/ ranch PB, Honey & Banana Tortilla Pinwheels Breaded Pork Chops, Parsley Potatoes, Peas	Cottage Cheese & Fruit Salami & Provolone Sandwich, Fruit, Pretzels Carrot Sticks Tortellini Soup, Bread	Smoothies, Egg, ham, cheese Bagels Grilled Turkey, avocado, feta, sun dried tomato Panini, Pickle, Chips Veggies & Ranch Dip Coconut Chicken, potatoes, veggies	Grilled Chicken Cesar Panini's Pickle Chips
Chicken Parmesan Breaded Chicken over pasta with marinara sauce), Salad, Bread Sticks	Egg, Sausage, Cheese Burrito & Fruit Turkey & Avocado Tortilla Wraps, Fruit String Cheese and fruit Beef Brisket, Mashed Potatoes, Corn or Peas	Smoothies, pancakes Sandwich, Pasta Salad, Fruit Parfait (layered yogurt, fruit, granola) Enchiladas or Beef Burritos, Rice, Beans, lettuce etc.	Smoothies, French Toast, Sausage Fish Sticks, veggies w/ ranch Frozen Gogurt Sliced cheese, meat, crackers Hot Taco Soup	Yogurt, Fruit, Granola Bologna Sandwich, fruit, pretzels Frozen Gogurt Homemade Calzones, Salad, Bread	Smoothies, Egg, ham, cheese scramble PB&J, fruit Trail Mix Breaded Chicken, baked potato, salad	Sloppy Joe's, Salad or Veggie

Meal Plan for: December

Use Shopping List D

Breakfast, Lunch, Snack, Dinner

Sun	Mon	Tue	Wed	Thu	Fri	Sat
Penne Pasta Bake, Bread, Salad	**Milk, Muffins & Fruit** Chicken Nuggets, Fruit, Nuts Grapes, Cheese chunks, Crackers Pork Tenderloin, Baked Potatoes, Salad	**Orange Smoothies, pancakes** Pizza Bites (French bread, pizza sauce, cheese, toppings) Pizzelle Cookies Taco Salad or Enchilada Casserole, Rice, Beans	**Smoothies, French Toast, Sausage** Fish Sticks, veggies w/ ranch dressing Apples & Peanut Butter Beef Stroganoff, Broccoli	**Yogurt, Fruit, Granola** Hot Dogs, Fruit, Chips Homemade Granola Bars Spiral Ham, Scallop Potatoes, Salad	**Green Smoothies Egg, ham, & cheese Bagels** Grilled Sandwiches: pesto, turkey, tomato, black olives, feta cheese Edible Christmas Trees Ham and white bean soup (Use leftover ham from Thur.)	Breaded Pork Chops, Mashed potatoes, Salad
Spaghetti, Meatballs, Salad, Bread	**Smoothies, pancakes** Grilled Cheese, Tomato Soup, Fruit White Chocolate Popcorn Breaded Chicken, Parsley Potatoes, Peas	**Smoothies, Eggs, Toast** Chicken Salad, Fruit (Or Cream cheese & Cucumber Sandwich) Soft Pretzels Grilled Chicken Quesadillas, Lettuce, tomato, guacamole, shredded cheese	**Smoothies, French Toast** Mac-n-Cheese, Veggies w/ ranch Parfait (layered yogurt, fruit, granola) Pork Roast, Sweet Potatoes, Green Beans	**Cottage Cheese & Fruit** Bologna Sandwich, Pretzels, Fruit Hot Chocolate, marshmallows and graham crackers BBQ Ribs, Corn, Mashed Potatoes	**Egg, ham, cheese Bagels** PB & Honey w/ banana sandwich, Fruit, Pretzels Sliced cheese, meat, crackers Homemade Pizza & Salad (or order for delivery)	BBQ sauce on Polska-Kielbasa Sausage Potatoes Broccoli
Ravioli or Rigatoni, Meatballs, Bread, Salad	**Milk, Muffins, Fruit** Grilled Ham, Cheese & Tomato, Fruit Sliced Apples with Peanut Butter Pork Chops, Breaded Cauliflower, Salad	**Smoothies, pancakes** Hamburgers Chips, Pickle Fruit Salsa & Tortilla Chips Creamy Chicken Burritos, Guacamole, Sour Cream, Cheese, Tomatoes, Lettuce etc.	**Smoothies, French Toast, Sausage** Mini Pizzas (French bread, pizza sauce, cheese, pepperoni) Cheese cubes w/ Pretzel toothpicks Crockpot Rotisserie Chicken, Potatoes, Veggie	**Yogurt, Fruit, Granola** Ham & Cream Cheese Tortilla Pinwheels, Snap Peas or Edamame Veggies & Ranch Dip Meatloaf, Mashed Potatoes, Salad or Veggie	**Smoothies, Egg, ham, cheese scramble** Egg Salad Sandwiches, Pretzels, Pickle Peppermint Bark Green Chili and Homemade Tortillas	Chicken Stir fry, Rice
Stuffed Shells, Salad, Bread	**Smoothies, Eggs, Toast** Tuna Salad Sandwich, Fruit, Cheese Sticks Cheese and Crackers Italian Beef Pot Roast & Veggies	**Smoothies, pancakes** Munchie Platter: Diced Cheese, Salami, Crackers, Fruit, Veggies Chex Mix Beef, Chicken Fajitas, Rice, Beans	**Smoothies, French Toast** Mac-n-Cheese, veggies w/ ranch PB, Honey & Banana Tortilla Pinwheels Breaded Pork Chops, Parsley Potatoes, Peas	**Cottage Cheese & Fruit** Salami & Provolone Sandwich, Fruit, Pretzels Carrot Sticks Tortellini Soup, Bread	**Smoothies, Egg, ham, cheese Bagels** Grilled Turkey, avocado, feta, sun dried tomato Panini, Pickle, Chips Veggies & Ranch Dip Coconut Chicken, potatoes, veggies	Grilled Chicken Cesar Panini's Pickle, Chips
Chicken Parmesan (Breaded Chicken over pasta with marinara sauce), Salad, Bread Sticks	**Egg, Sausage, Cheese Burrito & Fruit** Turkey & Avocado Tortilla Wraps & Fruit String Cheese and fruit Beef Brisket, Mashed Potatoes, Corn or Peas	**Smoothies, pancakes** Sandwich, Pasta Salad, Fruit Parfait (layered yogurt, fruit, granola) Enchiladas or Beef Burritos, Rice, Beans, Lettuce etc.	**Smoothies, French Toast, Sausage** Fish Sticks, veggies w/ ranch Sliced cheese, meat, crackers Hot Taco Soup	**Yogurt, Fruit, Granola** Bologna Sandwich, fruit, pretzels Frozen Gogurt Homemade Calzones, Salad, Bread	**Smoothies, Egg, ham, cheese scramble** PB&J, fruit Trail Mix Breaded Chicken, Baked Potato, Salad	Sloppy Joe's Salad or veggie

WEEKLY GROCERY LISTS

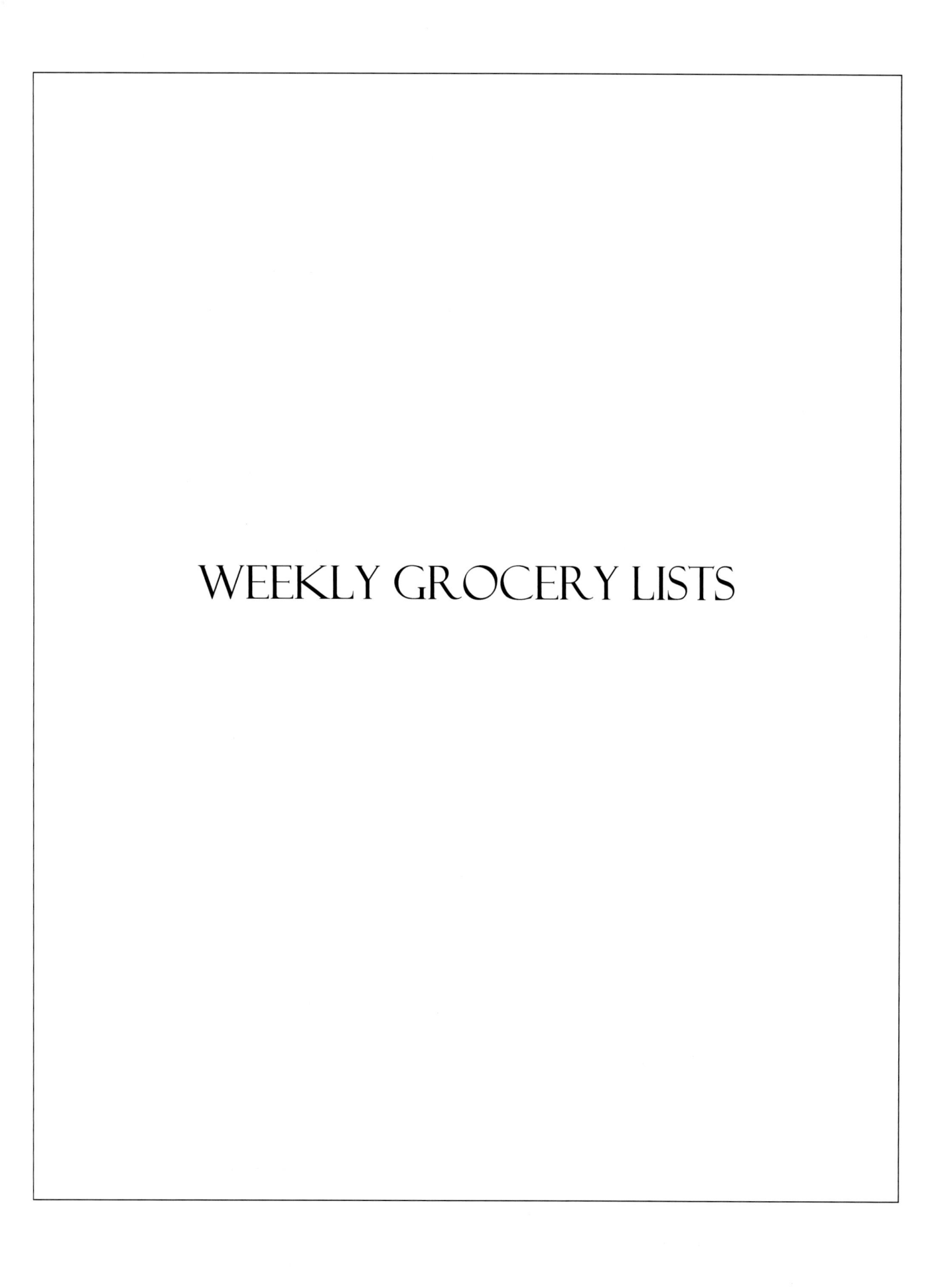

Shopping list: A week 1

Produce
- [ ] Lettuce
- [ ] Tomato
- [ ] Cucumber
- [ ] Avocado
- [ ] Strawberries
- [ ] Grapes
- [ ] Apples
- [ ] Potatoes
- [ ] Carrots
- [ ] Broccoli
- [ ] 1 onion
- [ ] Garlic
- [ ] Green onion
- [ ] Ginger
- [ ] Red bell pepper

Butcher/Deli
- [ ] Pork tenderloin
- [ ] 2 lbs. ground beef
- [ ] 1 lb. Flank Steak
- [ ] Hot dogs
- [ ] Spiral ham
- [ ] Deli ham
- [ ] Deli turkey
- [ ] Pepperoni, Ham pizza toppings
- [ ] 1 lb. flank steak or sirloin
- [ ] Chicken breasts or thighs (1, person)
- [ ] Bacon

Bakery
- [ ] Garlic bread
- [ ] Muffins
- [ ] Sandwich bread
- [ ] Bagels
- [ ] French bread
- [ ] Bread Bowls

Breakfast
- [ ] Cereal
- [ ] Granola
- [ ] Syrup

Dairy
- [ ] Milk
- [ ] Eggs
- [ ] Butter
- [ ] Half-n-half (2 meals)
- [ ] Cheese slices
- [ ] Pizza toppings
- [ ] Gogurt
- [ ] Yogurt
- [ ] Mozzarella, shredded
- [ ] Monterrey Jack cheese, shredded
- [ ] Shredded Cheddar cheese
- [ ] Feta cheese crumbles

Italian/Mexican
- [ ] Penne pasta
- [ ] Pizza sauce
- [ ] Black olives
- [ ] Salsa
- [ ] Rice
- [ ] Soy Sauce
- [ ] Tortillas
- [ ] Small can diced green chilies
- [ ] Red enchilada sauce

Baking/Spices
- [ ] Muffin Mix
- [ ] Pancake Mix
- [ ] Flour (whole wheat)
- [ ] Sugar
- [ ] Dark Brown Sugar
- [ ] Vegetable Oil
- [ ] Coconut oil
- [ ] Vanilla extract
- [ ] Taco seasoning
- [ ] Ground ginger
- [ ] Cinnamon
- [ ] Light brown sugar
- [ ] Corn Starch
- [ ] Quick cooking oats
- [ ] Pet evaporated milk

Soup/Canned
- [ ] Black Beans
- [ ] Chick peas
- [ ] Ranch Dressing
- [ ] Tortilla chip strips
- [ ] Chicken Broth (3 c.)
- [ ] Corn

Frozen
- [ ] Penne pasta
- [ ] Chicken nuggets
- [ ] Fish sticks
- [ ] Frozen corn
- [ ] Frozen broccoli
- [ ] Frozen fruit for smoothies
- [ ] _____
- [ ] _____

Snacks
- [ ] Crackers
- [ ] Mixed nuts
- [ ] _____

Beverages
- [ ] _____
- [ ] _____
- [ ] _____

Home Care
- [ ] _____
- [ ] _____
- [ ] _____

Other
- [ ] Honey
- [ ] Pesto sauce
- [ ] Peanut Butter
- [ ] _____

Shopping list: A week 2

Produce
- [ ] 1 yellow onion
- [ ] Lettuce
- [ ] Tomato
- [ ] Avocado
- [ ] Grapes
- [ ] Apples
- [ ] Pears
- [ ] Bananas
- [ ] Broccoli
- [ ] Carrots
- [ ] Cucumbers
- [ ] Potatoes

Butcher/Deli
- [ ] 1 lb. ground beef
- [ ] Chicken breast or thighs (1, person)
- [ ] Pork Butt Roast (approx.. 7lbs)
- [ ] Bologna
- [ ] Baby back ribs
- [ ] Summer sausage
- [ ] Pepperoni, sausage, ham (pizza toppings)
- [ ] Polska Kielbasa beef sausage
- [ ] _____

Bakery
- [ ] Garlic bread
- [ ] Sandwich bread
- [ ] Bagels
- [ ] Flour tortillas
- [ ] _____

Breakfast
- [ ] Syrup

Dairy
- [ ] Milk
- [ ] Eggs
- [ ] Butter
- [ ] Cream cheese spread
- [ ] 4 c. mozzarella, shredded
- [ ] Colby cheese sticks
- [ ] American cheese slices
- [ ] Nacho shredded cheese
- [ ] Plain yogurt
- [ ] Cottage cheese
- [ ] Pillsbury pizza dough
- [ ] _____

Italian/Mexican
- [ ] Penne pasta
- [ ] Tortillas
- [ ] Pizza Sauce
- [ ] _____

Baking/Spices
- [ ] Muffin mix
- [ ] Pancake mix
- [ ] White chocolate chips
- [ ] Craisins
- [ ] Bread crumbs
- [ ] 1 packet yeast
- [ ] Brown sugar
- [ ] Flour (whole wheat)
- [ ] Baking soda
- [ ] Granola
- [ ] Olive oil
- [ ] Garlic salt
- [ ] Onion salt
- [ ] Crushed pepper
- [ ] Parsley
- [ ] Marshmallows
- [ ] Basil
- [ ] Oregano

- [ ] Parsley

Soup/Canned
- [ ] 15 oz. Tomato Sauce w, Italian herbs
- [ ] 14.5 oz. can diced tomatoes in herbs
- [ ] 6 oz. can tomato paste w, roasted garlic
- [ ] Canned white chicken
- [ ] Tomato soup
- [ ] Mac-n-cheese
- [ ] Sweet potatoes

Frozen
- [ ] Fruit for smoothies
- [ ] Peas
- [ ] Green beans
- [ ] Corn
- [ ] Broccoli

Snacks
- [ ] Popcorn
- [ ] Pretzels
- [ ] Graham crackers

Beverages
- [ ] Hot chocolate mix

Home Care
- [ ] _____

Other
- [ ] Mayonnaise
- [ ] Ranch dressing
- [ ] BBQ Sauce
- [ ] Peanut butter
- [ ] Black olives (pizza topping)

Shopping list: A week 3

PRODUCE
- [ ] Apples
- [ ] Grapes
- [ ] 2 Kiwi
- [ ] 8 oz. Raspberries
- [ ] 1 lb. Strawberries
- [ ] ½ Cantaloupe
- [ ] Oranges
- [ ] Lettuce
- [ ] Tomatoes
- [ ] Broccoli
- [ ] Potatoes
- [ ] Cucumber
- [ ] Cauliflower
- [ ] Pickles
- [ ] Avocado
- [ ] 2 Yellow onions
- [ ] Garlic
- [ ] Carrots, julienned
- [ ] Carrots, whole

BUTCHER/DELI
- [ ] Pork Chops
- [ ] 3 lbs. Ground Beef
- [ ] Chicken Thighs (enough for 2 meals)
- [ ] Breakfast sausage links
- [ ] Pepperoni or Canadian bacon slices
- [ ] Whole Rotisserie Chicken
- [ ] Deli Ham or Turkey
- [ ] 1 ½ lbs. pork, cubed
- [ ]
- [ ] _____

BAKERY
- [ ] Bread
- [ ] Flour Tortillas
- [ ] French bread
- [ ] _____

BREAKFAST
- [ ] Syrup

DAIRY
- [ ] Milk
- [ ] Eggs
- [ ] Butter
- [ ] Cheese slices
- [ ] Sour Cream (low fat)
- [ ] Monterrey, Colby cheese, shredded
- [ ] Mozzarella cheese, shredded
- [ ] Cheddar cheese, shredded
- [ ] Colby Jack cheese block
- [ ] Yogurt
- [ ] Cream cheese spread
- [ ] Parmesan cheese, grated
- [ ] _____

ITALIAN/MEXICAN
- [ ] Rigatoni or Ravioli
- [ ] 27 oz. can green chili enchilada sauce
- [ ] Pizza sauce
- [ ] 2 sm. can diced green chili
- [ ] Tomato sauce
- [ ] Asian Stir-fry Seasoning
- [ ] Asian Stir Fry Sauce
- [ ] _____

BAKING/SPICES
- [ ] Craisins
- [ ] Walnuts
- [ ] Bread Crumbs
- [ ] Muffin Mix
- [ ] Cinnamon
- [ ] Sugar
- [ ] Oregano
- [ ] Basil
- [ ] Parsley
- [ ] Garlic Salt
- [ ] Onion Salt
- [ ] Cumin
- [ ] Parsley
- [ ] Dill weed
- [ ] Chives
- [ ] Brown sugar
- [ ] Flour
- [ ] Olive oil
- [ ] _____

SOUP/CANNED
- [ ] 1 10oz. can cream of chicken soup
- [ ] Instant White Rice
- [ ] _____

FROZEN
- [ ] Frozen Fruit for Smoothies
- [ ] Frozen edamame
- [ ] _____

SNACKS
- [ ] Pretzel sticks
- [ ] Granola
- [ ] _____

BEVERAGES
- [ ] _____
- [ ] _____
- [ ] _____

HOME CARE
- [ ] _____
- [ ] _____

OTHER
- [ ] Mayonnaise (lowfat)
- [ ] Ketchup
- [ ] Peanut Butter

Shopping list: A week 4

Produce
- [ ] Apples
- [ ] Oranges
- [ ] Strawberries
- [ ] 1 med. Onion
- [ ] Garlic cloves
- [ ] Lettuce
- [ ] Tomato
- [ ] Cucumber
- [ ] Avocado
- [ ] 1 Green bell pepper
- [ ] 1 Red bell pepper
- [ ] 2 med. onions
- [ ] Bananas
- [ ] Potatoes
- [ ] 1 Zucchini
- [ ] _____

Butcher/Deli
- [ ] 1 lb. ground beef
- [ ] Chicken or Steak for fajitas (thighs or sirloin)
- [ ] Chicken thighs (1 per, boneless, skinless)
- [ ] 1-2 chicken breasts
- [ ] Pork Chops (1 per.)
- [ ] Deli salami slices
- [ ] Sweet Italian Sausage links
- [ ] German Sausage links
- [ ] Deli turkey slices
- [ ] Pickles
- [ ] _____

Bakery
- [ ] Sandwich bread
- [ ] Flour tortillas
- [ ] French bread
- [ ] Bagels
- [ ] _____

Breakfast
- [ ] Syrup

Dairy
- [ ] Milk
- [ ] Eggs
- [ ] Butter
- [ ] Mozzarella, shredded
- [ ] Parmesan cheese, grated
- [ ] American cheese slices
- [ ] ½ c. ricotta cheese
- [ ] Cheese sticks
- [ ] Colby Jack cheese block
- [ ] Sour Cream
- [ ] Ranch dressing
- [ ] Cottage cheese
- [ ] Feta cheese, crumbled
- [ ] _____

Italian/Mexican
- [ ] 1 box Jumbo Shells
- [ ] 1 jars spaghetti sauce
- [ ] 1 sm. bag pinto beans
- [ ] _____

Baking/Spices
- [ ] Bread crumbs
- [ ] Parsley
- [ ] Olive oil
- [ ] Canola oil
- [ ] Oregano
- [ ] Basil
- [ ] Parsley
- [ ] Garlic salt
- [ ] Onion salt
- [ ] Italian seasoning
- [ ] Coconut flakes
- [ ] _____

Soup/Canned
- [ ] Canned Tuna
- [ ] Mac-n-cheese
- [ ] 2 10oz cans Beef broth
- [ ] 1 14 oz. can petite diced tomatoes
- [ ] 1 sm. can black olives, diced
- [ ] Sundried tomatoes
- [ ] _____

Frozen
- [ ] Frozen fruit for smoothies
- [ ] Peas
- [ ] Cheese tortellini
- [ ] Carrots, sliced
- [ ] _____
- [ ] _____

Snacks
- [ ] Chex mix
- [ ] Pretzels
- [ ] Baked chips
- [ ] _____

Beverages
- [ ] _____
- [ ] _____
- [ ] _____

Home Care
- [ ] _____
- [ ] _____

Other
- [ ] Peanut Butter
- [ ] Honey

Shopping list: A week 5

PRODUCE
- [ ] Apples
- [ ] Grapes
- [ ] Lettuce
- [ ] Tomato
- [ ] Cucumber
- [ ] Avocado
- [ ] Potatoes
- [ ] 3 Med. onion
- [ ] Carrots
- [ ] Celery
- [ ] Mushrooms
- [ ] _____

BUTCHER/DELI
- [ ] 4-6 chicken breasts (boneless, skinless)
- [ ] Chicken thighs (boneless, skinless 1per)
- [ ] Breakfast sausage, ground
- [ ] Breakfast sausage links
- [ ] Deli turkey slices
- [ ] 1 3lb. Beef brisket
- [ ] 3 lbs. ground beef
- [ ] Summer sausage link (for snack w, crackers)
- [ ] Bologna slices
- [ ] Canadian bacon slices
- [ ] Pepperoni slices
- [ ] Italian sausage, ground
- [ ] _____

BAKERY
- [ ] Sandwich bread
- [ ] Flour tortillas
- [ ] French bread
- [ ] Hamburger buns
- [ ] _____

BREAKFAST
- [ ] Syrup

DAIRY
- [ ] Milk
- [ ] Eggs
- [ ] Butter
- [ ] Parmesan cheese, grated
- [ ] Mozzarella cheese, shredded
- [ ] String cheese sticks
- [ ] Yogurt, vanilla
- [ ] Monterrey, Colby cheese, shredded
- [ ] Sour cream
- [ ] Colby Jack cheese block
- [ ] Gogurt
- [ ] _____

ITALIAN/MEXICAN
- [ ] Fettuccini
- [ ] Spirals (pasta salad)
- [ ] 27 oz. can green chili enchilada sauce
- [ ] Taco seasoning
- [ ] 1 jar marinara sauce
- [ ] _____

BAKING/SPICES
- [ ] Bread crumbs
- [ ] Olive oil
- [ ] Beef bouillon granules
- [ ] Pancake mix
- [ ] Garlic powder
- [ ] Chili powder
- [ ] Olive oil
- [ ] Brown sugar
- [ ] _____

SOUP/CANNED
- [ ] 6 oz. tomato paste
- [ ] 2 - 4.5 oz. diced tomatoes with roasted garlic
- [ ] 10oz. can black beans
- [ ] 10oz can pinto beans
- [ ] Instant white rice
- [ ] 1 10oz. can chicken broth
- [ ] 1 sm. can black olives, sliced
- [ ] _____

FROZEN
- [ ] Bread sticks, garlic
- [ ] Corn
- [ ] Peas
- [ ] Frozen fruit for smoothies
- [ ] Fish sticks
- [ ] Rhode's frozen bread dough
- [ ] _____
- [ ] _____

SNACKS
- [ ] Granola
- [ ] Crackers
- [ ] Fritos
- [ ] Pretzels
- [ ] Trail mix
- [ ] _____

BEVERAGES
- [ ] _____
- [ ] _____
- [ ] _____

HOME CARE
- [ ] _____
- [ ] _____

OTHER
- [ ] BBQ sauce
- [ ] Peanut butter
- [ ] Jelly
- [ ] Yellow mustard
- [ ] Ketchup
- [ ] Ranch dressing

Shopping list: B week 1

Produce
- [ ] Lettuce
- [ ] Tomato
- [ ] Cucumber
- [ ] Avocado
- [ ] Strawberries
- [ ] Grapes
- [ ] Apples
- [ ] Potatoes
- [ ] Carrots
- [ ] Broccoli
- [ ] 2 onion
- [ ] Garlic
- [ ] Green onion
- [ ] Ginger
- [ ] _____

Butcher/Deli
- [ ] Pork tenderloin
- [ ] 2 lbs. ground beef
- [ ] Hot dogs
- [ ] Spiral ham
- [ ] Deli ham
- [ ] Deli turkey
- [ ] Pepperoni, Ham pizza toppings
- [ ] 1 lb. flank steak or sirloin
- [ ] Chicken breasts or thighs (1, person)
- [ ] _____

Bakery
- [ ] Garlic bread
- [ ] Muffins
- [ ] Sandwich bread
- [ ] Bagels
- [ ] French bread

Breakfast
- [ ] Cereal
- [ ] Granola
- [ ] Syrup

Dairy
- [ ] Milk
- [ ] Eggs
- [ ] Butter
- [ ] Half-n-half (2 meals)
- [ ] Cheese slices
- [ ] Pizza toppings
- [ ] Gogurt
- [ ] Yogurt
- [ ] Mozzarella, shredded
- [ ] Monterrey Jack cheese, shredded
- [ ] Shredded Cheddar cheese
- [ ] Feta cheese crumbles

Italian/Mexican
- [ ] Penne pasta
- [ ] Wide Egg Noodles
- [ ] Pizza sauce
- [ ] Black olives
- [ ] Salsa
- [ ] Rice
- [ ] Soy Sauce
- [ ] Tortillas
- [ ] Small can diced green chilies
- [ ] Red enchilada sauce

Baking/Spices
- [ ] Muffin Mix
- [ ] Pancake Mix
- [ ] Flour (whole wheat)
- [ ] Sugar
- [ ] Vegetable Oil
- [ ] Coconut oil
- [ ] Vanilla extract
- [ ] Taco seasoning
- [ ] Ground ginger
- [ ] Cinnamon
- [ ] Light brown sugar
- [ ] Dark Brown Sugar
- [ ] Corn Starch
- [ ] Quick cooking oats
- [ ] Pet evaporated milk

Soup/Canned
- [ ] Black Beans
- [ ] Chick peas
- [ ] Ranch Dressing
- [ ] Tortilla chip strips
- [ ] Chicken Broth
- [ ] Brown Gravy Mix
- [ ] Canned Mushrooms
- [ ] _____

Frozen
- [ ] Penne pasta
- [ ] Chicken nuggets
- [ ] Fish sticks
- [ ] Frozen corn
- [ ] Frozen broccoli
- [ ] Frozen fruit for smoothies
- [ ] _____

Snacks
- [ ] Crackers
- [ ] Mixed nuts
- [ ] _____

Beverages
- [ ] _____
- [ ] _____
- [ ] _____

Home Care
- [ ] _____
- [ ] _____
- [ ] _____

Other
- [ ] Honey
- [ ] Pesto sauce
- [ ] Peanut Butter

Shopping list: B week 2

Produce
- [ ] 1 yellow onion
- [ ] Lettuce
- [ ] Cherry Tomatoes
- [ ] Avocado
- [ ] Grapes
- [ ] Apples
- [ ] Pears
- [ ] Bananas
- [ ] Broccoli
- [ ] Carrots
- [ ] Cucumbers
- [ ] Potatoes
- [ ] Zucchini
- [ ] Cherry Tomato
- [ ] Green Peppers
- [ ] Bell Pepper
- [ ] Yellow onion
- [ ] Mushrooms

Butcher/Deli
- [ ] 1 lb. ground beef
- [ ] Chicken breast or thighs (2 meals)
- [ ] Pork Butt Roast (approx.. 7lbs)
- [ ] Bologna
- [ ] Baby back ribs
- [ ] T-Bone Steaks
- [ ] Summer sausage
- [ ] _____

Bakery
- [ ] Garlic bread
- [ ] Sandwich bread
- [ ] Bagels
- [ ] Flour tortillas
- [ ] Hawaiian Rolls OR Hamburger Buns
- [ ] _____

Breakfast
- [ ] Syrup

Dairy
- [ ] Milk
- [ ] Eggs
- [ ] Butter
- [ ] Cream cheese spread
- [ ] 4 c. mozzarella, shredded
- [ ] Colby cheese sticks
- [ ] American cheese slices
- [ ] Nacho shredded cheese
- [ ] Plain yogurt
- [ ] Cottage cheese
- [ ] Grated Parmesan Cheese

Italian/Mexican
- [ ] Penne pasta
- [ ] Tortillas
- [ ] Ditilani or Elbow Macaroni
- [ ] _____

Baking/Spices
- [ ] Muffin mix
- [ ] Pancake mix
- [ ] White chocolate chips
- [ ] Craisins
- [ ] Bread crumbs
- [ ] 1 packet yeast
- [ ] Brown sugar
- [ ] Flour (whole wheat)
- [ ] Baking soda
- [ ] Granola
- [ ] Olive oil
- [ ] Garlic salt
- [ ] Onion salt
- [ ] Crushed pepper
- [ ] Parsley
- [ ] Basil
- [ ] Oregano
- [ ] Marshmallows

Soup/Canned
- [ ] 15 oz. Tomato Sauce w, Italian herbs
- [ ] 14.5 oz. can diced tomatoes in herbs
- [ ] 6 oz. can tomato paste w, roasted garlic
- [ ] Canned white chicken
- [ ] Tomato soup
- [ ] Mac-n-cheese
- [ ] Sweet potatoes
- [ ] Pork-n-beans or BBQ Beans

Frozen
- [ ] Fruit for smoothies
- [ ] Peas
- [ ] Green beans
- [ ] Corn
- [ ] Broccoli

Snacks
- [ ] Popcorn
- [ ] Pretzels
- [ ] Graham crackers

Beverages
- [ ] Hot chocolate mix

Home Care
- [ ] _____

Other
- [ ] Mayonnaise
- [ ] Ranch dressing
- [ ] BBQ Sauce
- [ ] Peanut butter
- [ ] BBQ Skewers
- [ ] BBQ Sauce

Shopping list: B week 3

Produce
- [ ] Apples
- [ ] Grapes
- [ ] 2 Kiwi
- [ ] 8 oz. Raspberries
- [ ] 1 lb. Strawberries
- [ ] ½ Cantaloupe
- [ ] Oranges
- [ ] Ice burg or green Lettuce
- [ ] Tomatoes
- [ ] Broccoli
- [ ] Potatoes
- [ ] Cucumber
- [ ] Carrots
- [ ] Cauliflower
- [ ] Pickles
- [ ] Avocado
- [ ] 2 Yellow onions
- [ ] Garlic
- [ ] Carrots, julienned
- [ ] Ginger, minced
- [ ] Green onion
- [ ] Cilantro (or sub. dried)
- [ ] Mushrooms
- [ ] Onion
- [ ] Bell Peppers
- [ ] Corn on Cob

Butcher/Deli
- [ ] Pork Chops
- [ ] 3 lbs. Ground Beef
- [ ] 6-8 Chicken Thighs
- [ ] Breakfast sausage links
- [ ] Pepperoni or Canadian bacon slices
- [ ] Deli Ham or Turkey
- [ ] 1 ½ lbs. pork, cubed
- [ ] Canadian bacon
- [ ] Pepperoni
- [ ] Sausage
- [ ] Roast Beef Slices
- [ ] Pasta Salad

Bakery
- [ ] Bread
- [ ] Flour Tortillas
- [ ] French bread
- [ ] Hoagie Rolls

Breakfast
- [ ] Syrup
- [ ] _____

Dairy
- [ ] Milk
- [ ] Eggs
- [ ] Butter
- [ ] Cheese slices
- [ ] Sour Cream (low fat)
- [ ] Monterrey, Colby cheese, shredded
- [ ] Mozzarella cheese, shredded
- [ ] Cheddar cheese, shredded
- [ ] Colby Jack cheese block
- [ ] Provolone Cheese Slices
- [ ] Yogurt
- [ ] Cream cheese spread
- [ ] Parmesan cheese, grated

Italian/Mexican
- [ ] Rigatoni or Ravioli
- [ ] 27 oz. can green chili enchilada sauce
- [ ] Pizza sauce
- [ ] 2 sm. can diced green chili
- [ ] Tomato sauce
- [ ] Asian Stir-fry Seasoning
- [ ] Asian Stir Fry Sauce
- [ ] 1 jar marinara sauce

Baking/Spices
- [ ] Muffin Mix
- [ ] Craisins
- [ ] Walnuts
- [ ] Cinnamon
- [ ] Sugar
- [ ] Oregano
- [ ] Basil
- [ ] Parsley
- [ ] Onion Salt
- [ ] Garlic Salt
- [ ] Cumin
- [ ] Flour
- [ ] Olive oil
- [ ] Soy Sauce
- [ ] Rice Vinegar
- [ ] Sesame Oil
- [ ] Crushed red pepper

Soup/Canned
- [ ] 1 10oz. can cream of chicken soup
- [ ] Instant White Rice
- [ ] Beef Consommé

Frozen
- [ ] Frozen Fruit for Smoothies
- [ ] Frozen edamame
- [ ] 1 loaf Rhode's frozen bread dough or Pillsbury pizza dough
- [ ] Frozen Peas/Carrots

Snacks
- [ ] Pretzel sticks
- [ ] Granola

Beverages
- [ ] _____
- [ ] _____

Other
- [ ] Mayonnaise (lowfat)
- [ ] Ketchup
- [ ] Peanut Butter

Shopping list: B week 4

Produce
- [ ] Apples
- [ ] Oranges
- [ ] Strawberries
- [ ] 1 med. Onion
- [ ] Garlic cloves
- [ ] Lettuce
- [ ] Tomato
- [ ] Cucumber
- [ ] Avocado
- [ ] 1 Green bell pepper
- [ ] 1 Red bell pepper
- [ ] 2 med. onions
- [ ] Bananas
- [ ] Potatoes
- [ ] 1 Zucchini
- [ ] _____

Butcher/Deli
- [ ] 2 lbs. ground beef
- [ ] Chicken or Steak for fajitas (thighs or sirloin)
- [ ] Chicken thighs (1 per, boneless, skinless)
- [ ] 1-2 chicken breasts
- [ ] Pork Chops (1 per.)
- [ ] Deli salami slices
- [ ] Sweet Italian Sausage links
- [ ] German Sausage links
- [ ] Deli turkey slices
- [ ] Pickles
- [ ] _____

Bakery
- [ ] Sandwich bread
- [ ] Flour tortillas
- [ ] French bread
- [ ] Bagels
- [ ] Hamburger Buns
- [ ] _____

Breakfast
- [ ] Syrup

Dairy
- [ ] Milk
- [ ] Eggs
- [ ] Butter
- [ ] Mozzarella, shredded
- [ ] Parmesan cheese, grated
- [ ] American cheese slices
- [ ] ½ c. ricotta cheese
- [ ] Cheese sticks
- [ ] Colby Jack cheese block
- [ ] Sour Cream
- [ ] Ranch dressing
- [ ] Cottage cheese
- [ ] Feta cheese, crumbled
- [ ] _____

Italian/Mexican
- [ ] 1 box Jumbo Shells
- [ ] 1 jars spaghetti sauce
- [ ] 1 sm. bag pinto beans
- [ ] _____

Baking/Spices
- [ ] Parsley
- [ ] Olive oil
- [ ] Canola oil
- [ ] Oregano
- [ ] Basil
- [ ] Parsley
- [ ] Garlic salt
- [ ] Onion salt
- [ ] Italian seasoning
- [ ] Coconut flakes
- [ ] _____

Soup/Canned
- [ ] Canned Tuna
- [ ] Mac-n-cheese
- [ ] 2 10oz cans Beef broth
- [ ] 1 14 oz. can petite diced tomatoes
- [ ] 1 sm. can black olives, diced
- [ ] Sundried tomatoes
- [ ] _____

Frozen
- [ ] Frozen fruit for smoothies
- [ ] Peas
- [ ] Cheese tortellini
- [ ] Carrots, sliced
- [ ] _____
- [ ] _____

Snacks
- [ ] Chex mix
- [ ] Pretzels
- [ ] Baked chips
- [ ] _____

Beverages
- [ ] _____
- [ ] _____
- [ ] _____

Home Care
- [ ] _____
- [ ] _____

Other
- [ ] Peanut Butter
- [ ] Honey
- [ ] Ketchup
- [ ] Mustard
- [ ] Relish

Shopping list: B week 5

Produce
- [ ] Apples
- [ ] Grapes
- [ ] Lettuce
- [ ] Tomato
- [ ] Cucumber
- [ ] Avocado
- [ ] Potatoes
- [ ] 3 Med. onion
- [ ] Carrots
- [ ] Celery
- [ ] Mushrooms
- [ ] Watermelon
- [ ] Onion
- [ ] _____

Butcher/Deli
- [ ] 4-6 chicken breasts (boneless, skinless)
- [ ] Chicken thighs (boneless, skinless 1per)
- [ ] Breakfast sausage, ground
- [ ] Breakfast sausage links
- [ ] Deli turkey slices
- [ ] 1 3lb. Beef brisket
- [ ] 3 lbs. ground beef
- [ ] Summer sausage link (for snack w, crackers)
- [ ] Bologna slices

Bakery
- [ ] Sandwich bread
- [ ] Flour tortillas
- [ ] French bread
- [ ] Hot dog buns
- [ ] _____

Breakfast
- [ ] Syrup

Dairy
- [ ] Milk
- [ ] Eggs
- [ ] Butter
- [ ] Parmesan cheese, grated
- [ ] Mozzarella cheese, shredded
- [ ] String cheese sticks
- [ ] Yogurt, vanilla
- [ ] Monterrey, Colby cheese, shredded
- [ ] Shredded Cheddar Cheese
- [ ] Sour cream
- [ ] Colby cheese block
- [ ] Gogurt

Italian/Mexican
- [ ] Fettuccini
- [ ] Spirals (pasta salad)
- [ ] 27 oz. can green chili enchilada sauce
- [ ] Taco seasoning
- [ ] _____

Baking/Spices
- [ ] Bread crumbs
- [ ] Olive oil
- [ ] Beef bouillon granules
- [ ] Pancake mix
- [ ] Garlic powder
- [ ] Chili powder
- [ ] Olive oil
- [ ] Brown sugar
- [ ] Cooking Spray

Soup/Canned
- [ ] 6 oz. tomato paste
- [ ] 2 - 4.5 oz. diced tomatoes with roasted garlic
- [ ] 10oz. can black beans
- [ ] 10oz can pinto beans
- [ ] Instant white rice
- [ ] 1 10oz. can chicken broth
- [ ] 1 sm. can black olives, sliced
- [ ] 1 can cream of mushroom soup

Frozen
- [ ] Bread sticks, garlic
- [ ] Corn
- [ ] Peas
- [ ] Frozen fruit for smoothies
- [ ] Fish sticks
- [ ] Rhode's frozen bread dough
- [ ] 1 bag tater tots

Snacks
- [ ] Granola
- [ ] Crackers
- [ ] Fritos
- [ ] Pretzels
- [ ] Trail mix
- [ ] _____

Beverages
- [ ] _____

Home Care
- [ ] _____

Other
- [ ] BBQ sauce
- [ ] Peanut butter
- [ ] Jelly
- [ ] Ranch dressing
- [ ] Yellow mustard
- [ ] Ketchup
- [ ] Worcestershire sauce

Shopping list: C week 1

PRODUCE
- [ ] Lettuce
- [ ] Tomato
- [ ] Cucumber
- [ ] Avocado
- [ ] Strawberries
- [ ] Grapes
- [ ] Apples
- [ ] Potatoes
- [ ] Carrots
- [ ] Broccoli
- [ ] 1 onion
- [ ] Garlic
- [ ] Green onion
- [ ] Red bell pepper

BUTCHER/DELI
- [ ] Pork tenderloin
- [ ] 2 lbs. ground beef
- [ ] Hot dogs
- [ ] Spiral ham
- [ ] Deli ham
- [ ] Deli turkey
- [ ] Pepperoni, Ham pizza toppings
- [ ] 1 lb. flank steak or sirloin
- [ ] Chicken breasts or thighs (1, person)
- [ ] _____

BAKERY
- [ ] Garlic bread
- [ ] Muffins
- [ ] Sandwich bread
- [ ] Bagels
- [ ] French bread

BREAKFAST
- [ ] Cereal
- [ ] Granola
- [ ] Syrup

DAIRY
- [ ] Milk
- [ ] Eggs
- [ ] Butter
- [ ] Half-n-half (2 meals)
- [ ] Cheese slices
- [ ] Pizza toppings
- [ ] Gogurt
- [ ] Yogurt
- [ ] Mozzarella, shredded
- [ ] Monterrey Jack cheese, shredded
- [ ] Shredded Cheddar cheese
- [ ] Feta cheese crumbles

ITALIAN/MEXICAN
- [ ] Penne pasta
- [ ] Pizza sauce
- [ ] Black olives
- [ ] Salsa
- [ ] Rice
- [ ] Soy Sauce
- [ ] Tortillas
- [ ] Small can diced green chilies
- [ ] Red enchilada sauce

BAKING/SPICES
- [ ] Muffin Mix
- [ ] Pancake Mix
- [ ] Flour (whole wheat & white)
- [ ] Sugar
- [ ] Oil
- [ ] Coconut oil
- [ ] Vanilla extract
- [ ] Taco seasoning
- [ ] Ground ginger
- [ ] Cinnamon
- [ ] Light brown sugar
- [ ] Corn Starch
- [ ] Quick cooking oats
- [ ] Pet evaporated milk

SOUP/CANNED
- [ ] Black Beans
- [ ] Chick peas
- [ ] Tortilla chip strips
- [ ] Chicken Broth (3 c.)
- [ ] Corn

FROZEN
- [ ] Penne pasta
- [ ] Chicken nuggets
- [ ] Fish sticks
- [ ] Frozen corn
- [ ] Frozen broccoli
- [ ] Frozen fruit for smoothies
- [ ] _____
- [ ] _____

SNACKS
- [ ] Crackers
- [ ] Mixed nuts
- [ ] _____

BEVERAGES
- [ ] _____
- [ ] _____
- [ ] _____

HOME CARE
- [ ] _____
- [ ] _____
- [ ] _____

OTHER
- [ ] Honey
- [ ] Pesto sauce
- [ ] Peanut Butter
- [ ] Ranch Dressing
- [ ] _____

Shopping list: C week 2

PRODUCE

- [ ] 1 yellow onion
- [ ] Lettuce
- [ ] Tomato
- [ ] Avocado
- [ ] Grapes
- [ ] Apples
- [ ] Pears
- [ ] Bananas
- [ ] Broccoli
- [ ] Carrots
- [ ] Cucumbers
- [ ] Potatoes

BUTCHER/DELI

- [ ] 1 lb. ground beef
- [ ] Chicken breast or thighs (1, person)
- [ ] Pork Butt Roast (approx.. 7lbs)
- [ ] Bologna
- [ ] Baby back ribs
- [ ] Summer sausage
- [ ] Pepperoni, sausage, ham (pizza toppings)
- [ ] Polska Kielbasa beef sausage
- [ ] _____

BAKERY

- [ ] Garlic bread
- [ ] Sandwich bread
- [ ] Bagels
- [ ] Flour tortillas
- [ ] _____

BREAKFAST

- [ ] Syrup

DAIRY

- [ ] Milk
- [ ] Eggs
- [ ] Butter
- [ ] Cream cheese spread
- [ ] 4 c. mozzarella, shredded
- [ ] Colby cheese sticks
- [ ] American cheese slices
- [ ] Nacho shredded cheese
- [ ] Plain yogurt
- [ ] Cottage cheese
- [ ] Pillsbury pizza dough
- [ ] Grated Parmesan Cheese

ITALIAN/MEXICAN

- [ ] Penne pasta
- [ ] Tortillas
- [ ] Pizza Sauce
- [ ] _____

BAKING/SPICES

- [ ] Muffin mix
- [ ] Pancake mix
- [ ] White chocolate chips
- [ ] Craisins
- [ ] Bread crumbs
- [ ] 1 packet yeast
- [ ] Brown sugar
- [ ] Flour (whole wheat)
- [ ] Baking soda
- [ ] Granola
- [ ] Olive oil
- [ ] Garlic salt
- [ ] Onion salt
- [ ] Crushed pepper
- [ ] Parsley
- [ ] Basil
- [ ] Oregano
- [ ] Marshmallows

SOUP/CANNED

- [ ] 15 oz. Tomato Sauce w, Italian herbs
- [ ] 14.5 oz. can diced tomatoes in herbs
- [ ] 6 oz. can tomato paste w, roasted garlic
- [ ] Canned white chicken
- [ ] Tomato soup
- [ ] Mac-n-cheese
- [ ] Sweet potatoes

FROZEN

- [ ] Fruit for smoothies
- [ ] Peas
- [ ] Green beans
- [ ] Corn
- [ ] Broccoli

SNACKS

- [ ] Popcorn
- [ ] Pretzels
- [ ] Graham crackers

BEVERAGES

- [ ] Hot chocolate mix

HOME CARE

- [ ] _____

OTHER

- [ ] Mayonnaise
- [ ] Ranch dressing
- [ ] BBQ Sauce
- [ ] Peanut butter
- [ ] Black olives (pizza topping)

Shopping list: C week 3

Produce
- [ ] Apples
- [ ] Grapes
- [ ] 2 Kiwi
- [ ] 8 oz. Raspberries
- [ ] 1 lb. Strawberries
- [ ] ½ Cantaloupe
- [ ] Oranges
- [ ] Lettuce
- [ ] Tomatoes
- [ ] Broccoli
- [ ] Potatoes
- [ ] Cucumber
- [ ] Cauliflower
- [ ] Pickles
- [ ] Avocado
- [ ] 2 Yellow onions
- [ ] Garlic
- [ ] Carrots, julienned
- [ ] _____

Butcher/Deli
- [ ] Pork Chops
- [ ] 3 lbs. Ground Beef
- [ ] Chicken Thighs (enough for 2 meals)
- [ ] Breakfast sausage links
- [ ] Pepperoni or Canadian bacon slices
- [ ] Whole Rotisserie Chicken
- [ ] Deli Ham or Turkey
- [ ] 1 ½ lbs. pork, cubed
- [ ] _____
- [ ] _____

Bakery
- [ ] Bread
- [ ] Flour Tortillas
- [ ] French bread
- [ ] _____

Breakfast
- [ ] Syrup

Dairy
- [ ] Milk
- [ ] Eggs
- [ ] Butter
- [ ] Cheese slices
- [ ] Sour Cream (low fat)
- [ ] Monterrey, Colby cheese, shredded
- [ ] Mozzarella cheese, shredded
- [ ] Cheddar cheese, shredded
- [ ] Colby Jack cheese block
- [ ] Yogurt
- [ ] Cream cheese spread
- [ ] Parmesan cheese, grated
- [ ] _____

Italian/Mexican
- [ ] Rigatoni or Ravioli
- [ ] 27 oz. can green chili enchilada sauce
- [ ] Pizza sauce
- [ ] 2 sm. can diced green chili
- [ ] Tomato sauce
- [ ] Asian Stir-fry Seasoning
- [ ] Asian Stir Fry Sauce
- [ ] _____

Baking/Spices
- [ ] Craisins
- [ ] Walnuts
- [ ] _____
- [ ] Bread Crumbs
- [ ] Muffin Mix
- [ ] Cinnamon
- [ ] Sugar
- [ ] Oregano
- [ ] Basil
- [ ] Garlic Salt
- [ ] Onion Salt
- [ ] Cumin
- [ ] Parsley
- [ ] Dill weed
- [ ] Chives
- [ ] Brown sugar
- [ ] Flour
- [ ] Olive oil
- [ ] _____

Soup/Canned
- [ ] 1 10oz. can cream of chicken soup
- [ ] Instant White Rice
- [ ] _____

Frozen
- [ ] Frozen Fruit for Smoothies
- [ ] Frozen edamame
- [ ] _____

Snacks
- [ ] Pretzel sticks
- [ ] Granola
- [ ] _____

Beverages
- [ ] _____
- [ ] _____
- [ ] _____

Home Care
- [ ] _____
- [ ] _____

Other
- [ ] Mayonnaise (lowfat)
- [ ] Ketchup
- [ ] Peanut Butter

Shopping list: C week 4

Produce
- [ ] Apples
- [ ] Oranges
- [ ] Strawberries
- [ ] 1 med. Onion
- [ ] Garlic cloves
- [ ] Lettuce
- [ ] Tomato
- [ ] Cucumber
- [ ] Avocado
- [ ] 1 Green bell pepper
- [ ] 1 Red bell pepper
- [ ] 2 med. onions
- [ ] Bananas
- [ ] Potatoes
- [ ] 1 Zucchini
- [ ] _____

Butcher/Deli
- [ ] 1 lb. ground beef
- [ ] Chicken or Steak for fajitas (thighs or sirloin)
- [ ] Chicken thighs (1 per, boneless, skinless)
- [ ] 1-2 chicken breasts
- [ ] Pork Chops (1 per.)
- [ ] Deli salami slices
- [ ] Sweet Italian Sausage links
- [ ] German Sausage links
- [ ] Deli turkey slices
- [ ] Pickles
- [ ] _____

Bakery
- [ ] Sandwich bread
- [ ] Flour tortillas
- [ ] French bread
- [ ] Bagels
- [ ] _____

Breakfast
- [ ] Syrup

Dairy
- [ ] Milk
- [ ] Eggs
- [ ] Butter
- [ ] Mozzarella, shredded
- [ ] Parmesan cheese, grated
- [ ] American cheese slices
- [ ] ½ c. ricotta cheese
- [ ] Cheese sticks
- [ ] Cheese block
- [ ] Sour Cream
- [ ] Cottage cheese
- [ ] Feta cheese, crumbled
- [ ] _____

Italian/Mexican
- [ ] 1 box Jumbo Shells
- [ ] 1 jars spaghetti sauce
- [ ] 1 sm. bag pinto beans
- [ ] _____

Baking/Spices
- [ ] Bread crumbs
- [ ] Parsley
- [ ] Olive oil
- [ ] Canola oil
- [ ] Oregano
- [ ] Basil
- [ ] Parsley
- [ ] Garlic salt
- [ ] Onion salt
- [ ] Italian seasoning
- [ ] Coconut flakes
- [ ] _____

Soup/Canned
- [ ] Canned Tuna
- [ ] Mac-n-cheese
- [ ] 2 10oz cans Beef broth
- [ ] 1 14 oz. can petite diced tomatoes
- [ ] 1 sm. can black olives, diced
- [ ] Sundried tomatoes
- [ ] _____

Frozen
- [ ] Frozen fruit for smoothies
- [ ] Peas
- [ ] Cheese tortellini
- [ ] Carrots, sliced
- [ ] _____
- [ ] _____

Snacks
- [ ] Chex mix
- [ ] Pretzels
- [ ] Baked chips
- [ ] _____

Beverages
- [ ] _____
- [ ] _____
- [ ] _____

Home Care
- [ ] _____
- [ ] _____

Other
- [ ] Peanut Butter
- [ ] Honey
- [ ] Ranch dressing

Shopping list: C week 5

Produce
- [ ] Apples
- [ ] Grapes
- [ ] Lettuce
- [ ] Tomato
- [ ] Cucumber
- [ ] Avocado
- [ ] Potatoes
- [ ] 3 Med. onion
- [ ] Carrots
- [ ] Celery
- [ ] Mushrooms
- [ ] _____

Butcher/Deli
- [ ] 4-6 chicken breasts (boneless, skinless)
- [ ] Chicken thighs (boneless, skinless 1per)
- [ ] Breakfast sausage, ground
- [ ] Breakfast sausage links
- [ ] Deli turkey slices
- [ ] 1 3lb. Beef brisket
- [ ] 3 lbs. ground beef
- [ ] Summer sausage link (for snack w, crackers)
- [ ] Bologna slices
- [ ] Canadian bacon slices
- [ ] Pepperoni slices
- [ ] Italian sausage, ground

Bakery
- [ ] Sandwich bread
- [ ] Flour tortillas
- [ ] French bread
- [ ] Hamburger buns

Breakfast
- [ ] Syrup

Dairy
- [ ] Milk
- [ ] Eggs
- [ ] Butter
- [ ] Parmesan cheese, grated
- [ ] Mozzarella cheese, shredded
- [ ] String cheese sticks
- [ ] Yogurt, vanilla
- [ ] Monterrey, Colby cheese, shredded
- [ ] Sour cream
- [ ] Colby cheese block
- [ ] Gogurt
- [ ] _____

Italian/Mexican
- [ ] Fettuccini
- [ ] Spirals (pasta salad)
- [ ] 27 oz. can green chili enchilada sauce
- [ ] Taco seasoning
- [ ] 1 jar marinara sauce
- [ ] _____

Baking/Spices
- [ ] Bread crumbs
- [ ] Olive oil
- [ ] Beef bouillon granules
- [ ] Pancake mix
- [ ] Garlic powder
- [ ] Chili powder
- [ ] Olive oil
- [ ] Brown sugar

Soup/Canned
- [ ] 6 oz. tomato paste
- [ ] 2 - 4.5 oz. diced tomatoes with roasted garlic
- [ ] 10z. can black beans
- [ ] 10oz can pinto beans
- [ ] Instant white rice
- [ ] 1 10oz. can chicken broth
- [ ] 1 sm. can black olives, sliced

Frozen
- [ ] Bread sticks, garlic
- [ ] Corn
- [ ] Peas
- [ ] Frozen fruit for smoothies
- [ ] Fish sticks
- [ ] Rhode's frozen bread dough
- [ ] _____

Snacks
- [ ] Granola
- [ ] Crackers
- [ ] Fritos
- [ ] Pretzels
- [ ] Trail mix
- [ ] _____

Beverages
- [ ] _____

Home Care
- [ ] _____

Other
- [ ] BBQ sauce
- [ ] Peanut butter
- [ ] Jelly
- [ ] Ranch dressing
- [ ] Yellow mustard
- [ ] Ketchup

Shopping list: D week 1

PRODUCE
- [ ] Lettuce
- [ ] Tomato
- [ ] Cucumber
- [ ] Avocado
- [ ] Strawberries
- [ ] Grapes
- [ ] Apples
- [ ] Potatoes
- [ ] Carrots
- [ ] Broccoli
- [ ] 2 onions
- [ ] Garlic
- [ ] Green onion
- [ ] Baby Spinach Leaves
- [ ] Bananas
- [ ] Lemon

BUTCHER/DELI
- [ ] Pork tenderloin
- [ ] 2 lbs. ground beef
- [ ] Hot dogs
- [ ] Spiral ham
- [ ] Deli ham
- [ ] Deli turkey
- [ ] Pepperoni, Ham pizza toppings
- [ ] 1 lb. flank steak or sirloin
- [ ] Chicken breasts or thighs (1, person)

BAKERY
- [ ] Garlic bread
- [ ] Muffins
- [ ] Sandwich bread
- [ ] Bagels
- [ ] French bread

BREAKFAST
- [ ] Cereal
- [ ] Granola
- [ ] Syrup

DAIRY
- [ ] Milk
- [ ] Orange Juice
- [ ] 2 dozen Eggs
- [ ] Butter
- [ ] 2 sticks Margarine
- [ ] Half-n-half (2 meals)
- [ ] Cheese slices
- [ ] Pizza toppings
- [ ] Gogurt
- [ ] Yogurt
- [ ] Mozzarella, shredded
- [ ] Monterrey Jack cheese, shredded
- [ ] Shredded Cheddar cheese
- [ ] Feta cheese crumbles

ITALIAN/MEXICAN
- [ ] Penne pasta
- [ ] Wide Egg Noodles
- [ ] Pizza sauce
- [ ] Black olives
- [ ] Salsa
- [ ] Rice
- [ ] Soy Sauce
- [ ] Tortillas
- [ ] Small can diced green chilies
- [ ] Red enchilada sauce

BAKING/SPICES
- [ ] Muffin mix
- [ ] Pancake mix
- [ ] Flour (whole wheat)
- [ ] Sugar
- [ ] Oil
- [ ] Baking powder
- [ ] Coconut oil
- [ ] Vanilla extract
- [ ] Taco seasoning
- [ ] Ground ginger
- [ ] Cinnamon
- [ ] Light brown sugar
- [ ] Corn Starch

- [ ] Quick cooking oats
- [ ] Pet evaporated milk
- [ ] Powdered Sugar
- [ ] Sugar Ice Cream Cones
- [ ] Green Frosting
- [ ] Sprinkles

SOUP/CANNED
- [ ] Black Beans
- [ ] Chick peas
- [ ] Tortilla chip strips
- [ ] Chicken Broth
- [ ] Brown Gravy
- [ ] Mushroom pieces

FROZEN
- [ ] Penne pasta
- [ ] Chicken nuggets
- [ ] Fish sticks
- [ ] Frozen corn
- [ ] Frozen broccoli
- [ ] Frozen fruit for smoothies

SNACKS
- [ ] Crackers
- [ ] Mixed nuts

BEVERAGES
- [ ] _____

OTHER
- [ ] Honey
- [ ] Pesto sauce
- [ ] Peanut Butter
- [ ] Ranch Dressing

Shopping list: D week 2

PRODUCE
- [ ] 1 yellow onion
- [ ] Potatoes

BUTCHER/DELI
- [ ] 1 lb. ground beef
- [ ] Chicken breast or thighs (1, person)
- [ ] Pork Butt Roast (approx.. 7lbs)
- [ ] Bologna
- [ ] Baby back ribs
- [ ] Summer sausage
- [ ] Pepperoni, sausage, ham (pizza toppings)
- [ ] Polska Kielbasa beef sausage
- [ ] _____

BAKERY
- [ ] Garlic bread
- [ ] Sandwich bread
- [ ] Bagels
- [ ] Flour tortillas
- [ ] _____

BREAKFAST
- [ ] Syrup

DAIRY
- [ ] Milk
- [ ] Eggs
- [ ] Butter
- [ ] Cream cheese spread
- [ ] 4 c. mozzarella, shredded
- [ ] Colby cheese sticks
- [ ] American cheese slices
- [ ] Nacho shredded cheese
- [ ] Plain yogurt
- [ ] Cottage cheese
- [ ] Pillsbury pizza dough
- [ ] Grated Parmesan Cheese

ITALIAN/MEXICAN
- [ ] Penne pasta
- [ ] Tortillas
- [ ] Pizza Sauce
- [ ] _____

BAKING/SPICES
- [ ] Muffin mix
- [ ] Pancake mix
- [ ] White chocolate chips
- [ ] Craisins
- [ ] Bread crumbs
- [ ] 1 packet yeast
- [ ] Brown sugar
- [ ] Flour (whole wheat)
- [ ] Baking soda
- [ ] Granola
- [ ] Olive oil
- [ ] Garlic salt
- [ ] Onion salt
- [ ] Basil
- [ ] Oregano
- [ ] Crushed pepper
- [ ] Parsley
- [ ] Marshmallows
- [ ] White Chocolate Chips

SOUP/CANNED
- [ ] 15 oz. Tomato Sauce w, Italian herbs
- [ ] 14.5 oz. can diced tomatoes in herbs
- [ ] 6 oz. can tomato paste w, roasted garlic
- [ ] Canned white chicken
- [ ] Tomato soup
- [ ] Mac-n-cheese
- [ ] Sweet potatoes

FROZEN
- [ ] Fruit for smoothies
- [ ] Peas
- [ ] Green beans
- [ ] Corn
- [ ] Broccoli

SNACKS
- [ ] Popcorn
- [ ] Pretzels
- [ ] Graham crackers

BEVERAGES
- [ ] Hot chocolate mix

HOME CARE
- [ ] _____

OTHER
- [ ] Mayonnaise
- [ ] Ranch dressing
- [ ] BBQ Sauce
- [ ] Peanut butter
- [ ] Black olives (pizza topping)

Shopping list: D week 3

Produce
- ☐ Apples
- ☐ Grapes
- ☐ 2 Kiwi
- ☐ 8 oz. Raspberries
- ☐ 1 lb. Strawberries
- ☐ ½ Cantaloupe
- ☐ Oranges
- ☐ Lettuce
- ☐ Tomatoes
- ☐ Broccoli
- ☐ Potatoes
- ☐ Cucumber
- ☐ Cauliflower
- ☐ Pickles
- ☐ Avocado
- ☐ 2 Yellow onions
- ☐ Garlic
- ☐ Carrots, julienned
- ☐ Carrots, whole

Butcher/Deli
- ☐ Pork chops
- ☐ 3 lbs. ground beef
- ☐ Chicken thighs (enough for 2 meals)
- ☐ Breakfast sausage links
- ☐ Pepperoni or Canadian bacon slices
- ☐ Whole rotisserie chicken
- ☐ Deli ham or turkey
- ☐ 1 ½ lbs. pork, cubed

Bakery
- ☐ Bread
- ☐ Flour Tortillas
- ☐ French bread

Breakfast
- ☐ Syrup
- ☐ _____

Dairy
- ☐ Milk
- ☐ Eggs
- ☐ Butter
- ☐ Cheese slices
- ☐ Sour Cream (low fat)
- ☐ Monterrey, Colby cheese, shredded
- ☐ Mozzarella cheese, shredded
- ☐ Cheddar cheese, shredded
- ☐ Colby Jack cheese block
- ☐ Yogurt
- ☐ Cream cheese spread
- ☐ Parmesan cheese, grated

Italian/Mexican
- ☐ Rigatoni or Ravioli
- ☐ 27 oz. can green chili enchilada sauce
- ☐ Pizza sauce
- ☐ 2 sm. can diced green chili
- ☐ Tomato sauce
- ☐ Asian Stir-fry Seasoning
- ☐ Asian Stir Fry Sauce

Baking/Spices
- ☐ Craisins
- ☐ Bread Crumbs
- ☐ Muffin Mix
- ☐ Cinnamon
- ☐ Sugar
- ☐ Oregano
- ☐ Basil
- ☐ Cumin
- ☐ Parsley
- ☐ Garlic Salt
- ☐ Onion Salt
- ☐ Dill weed
- ☐ Chives
- ☐ Brown sugar
- ☐ Flour
- ☐ Olive oil
- ☐ White Chocolate Chips
- ☐ Peppermint Extract
- ☐ Semisweet Chocolate Chips
- ☐ Candy Canes Crushed
- ☐ Cooking Spray

Soup/Canned
- ☐ 1 10oz. can cream of chicken soup
- ☐ Instant White Rice
- ☐ _____

Frozen
- ☐ Frozen Fruit for Smoothies
- ☐ Frozen edamame
- ☐ _____

Snacks
- ☐ Pretzel sticks
- ☐ Granola
- ☐ _____

Beverages
- ☐ _____
- ☐ _____

Home Care
- ☐ _____
- ☐ _____

Other
- ☐ Mayonnaise (lowfat)
- ☐ Ketchup
- ☐ Peanut butter
- ☐ Aluminum foil

Shopping list: D week 4

Produce
- [ ] Apples
- [ ] Oranges
- [ ] Strawberries
- [ ] 1 med. Onion
- [ ] Garlic cloves
- [ ] Lettuce
- [ ] Tomato
- [ ] Cucumber
- [ ] Avocado
- [ ] 1 Green bell pepper
- [ ] 1 Red bell pepper
- [ ] 2 med. onions
- [ ] Bananas
- [ ] Potatoes
- [ ] 1 Zucchini
- [ ] _____

Butcher/Deli
- [ ] 1 lb. ground beef
- [ ] Chicken or Steak for fajitas (thighs or sirloin)
- [ ] Chicken thighs (1 per, boneless, skinless)
- [ ] 1-2 chicken breasts
- [ ] Pork Chops (1 per.)
- [ ] Deli salami slices
- [ ] Sweet Italian Sausage links
- [ ] German Sausage links
- [ ] Deli turkey slices
- [ ] Pickles
- [ ] _____

Bakery
- [ ] Sandwich bread
- [ ] Flour tortillas
- [ ] French bread
- [ ] Bagels
- [ ] _____

Breakfast
- [ ] Syrup

Dairy
- [ ] Milk
- [ ] Eggs
- [ ] Butter
- [ ] Mozzarella, shredded
- [ ] Parmesan cheese, grated
- [ ] American cheese slices
- [ ] ½ c. ricotta cheese
- [ ] Cheese sticks
- [ ] Colby Jack cheese block
- [ ] Sour Cream
- [ ] Cottage cheese
- [ ] Feta cheese, crumbled
- [ ] _____

Italian/Mexican
- [ ] 1 box Jumbo Shells
- [ ] 1 jars spaghetti sauce
- [ ] 1 sm. bag pinto beans
- [ ] _____

Baking/Spices
- [ ] Bread crumbs
- [ ] Parsley
- [ ] Olive oil
- [ ] Canola oil
- [ ] Oregano
- [ ] Basil
- [ ] Parsley
- [ ] Garlic salt
- [ ] Onion salt
- [ ] Italian seasoning
- [ ] Coconut flakes
- [ ] _____

Soup/Canned
- [ ] Canned Tuna
- [ ] Mac-n-cheese
- [ ] 2 10oz cans Beef broth
- [ ] 1 14 oz. can petite diced tomatoes
- [ ] 1 sm. can black olives, diced
- [ ] Sundried tomatoes
- [ ] _____

Frozen
- [ ] Frozen fruit for smoothies
- [ ] Peas
- [ ] Cheese tortellini
- [ ] Carrots, sliced
- [ ] _____
- [ ] _____

Snacks
- [ ] Chex mix
- [ ] Pretzels
- [ ] Baked chips
- [ ] _____

Beverages
- [ ] _____
- [ ] _____
- [ ] _____

Home Care
- [ ] _____
- [ ] _____

Other
- [ ] Peanut Butter
- [ ] Honey
- [ ] Ranch dressing

Shopping list: D week 5

Produce
- [ ] Apples
- [ ] Grapes
- [ ] Lettuce
- [ ] Tomato
- [ ] Cucumber
- [ ] Avocado
- [ ] Potatoes
- [ ] 3 Med. onion
- [ ] Carrots
- [ ] Celery
- [ ] Mushrooms
- [ ] _____

Butcher/Deli
- [ ] 4-6 chicken breasts (boneless, skinless)
- [ ] Chicken thighs (boneless, skinless 1per)
- [ ] Breakfast sausage, ground
- [ ] Breakfast sausage links
- [ ] Deli turkey slices
- [ ] 1 3lb. Beef brisket
- [ ] 3 lbs. ground beef
- [ ] Summer sausage link (for snack w, crackers)
- [ ] Bologna slices
- [ ] Canadian bacon slices
- [ ] Pepperoni slices
- [ ] Italian sausage, ground

Bakery
- [ ] Sandwich bread
- [ ] Flour tortillas
- [ ] French bread
- [ ] Hamburger buns
- [ ] _____

Breakfast
- [ ] Syrup

Dairy
- [ ] Milk
- [ ] Eggs
- [ ] Butter
- [ ] Parmesan cheese, grated
- [ ] Mozzarella cheese, shredded
- [ ] String cheese sticks
- [ ] Yogurt, vanilla
- [ ] Monterrey, Colby cheese, shredded
- [ ] Sour cream
- [ ] Colby cheese block
- [ ] Gogurt

Italian/Mexican
- [ ] Fettuccini
- [ ] Wide egg noodles
- [ ] Spirals (pasta salad)
- [ ] 27 oz. can green chili enchilada sauce
- [ ] Taco seasoning
- [ ] 1 jar marinara sauce

Baking/Spices
- [ ] Bread crumbs
- [ ] Olive oil
- [ ] Beef bouillon granules
- [ ] Pancake mix
- [ ] Garlic powder
- [ ] Chili powder
- [ ] Olive oil
- [ ] Brown sugar

Soup/Canned
- [ ] 6 oz. tomato paste
- [ ] 2 - 4.5 oz. diced tomatoes with roasted garlic
- [ ] 10oz. can black beans
- [ ] 10oz can pinto beans
- [ ] Instant white rice
- [ ] 1 10oz. can chicken broth
- [ ] 1 sm. can black olives, sliced
- [ ] Mushroom pieces
- [ ] Brown Gravy

Frozen
- [ ] Bread sticks, garlic
- [ ] Corn
- [ ] Peas
- [ ] Frozen fruit for smoothies
- [ ] Fish sticks
- [ ] Rhode's frozen bread dough

Snacks
- [ ] Granola
- [ ] Crackers
- [ ] Fritos
- [ ] Pretzels
- [ ] Trail mix

Beverages
- [ ] _____
- [ ] _____

Home Care
- [ ] _____

Other
- [ ] BBQ sauce
- [ ] Peanut butter
- [ ] Jelly
- [ ] Yellow mustard
- [ ] Ketchup
- [ ] Ranch dressing

Shopping list: _____

Produce
- [ ] _____
- [ ] _____
- [ ] _____
- [ ] _____
- [ ] _____
- [ ] _____
- [ ] _____
- [ ] _____
- [ ] _____
- [ ] _____

Dairy
- [ ] _____
- [ ] _____
- [ ] _____
- [ ] _____
- [ ] _____
- [ ] _____
- [ ] _____
- [ ] _____
- [ ] _____
- [ ] _____

Frozen
- [ ] _____
- [ ] _____
- [ ] _____
- [ ] _____
- [ ] _____
- [ ] _____
- [ ] _____
- [ ] _____
- [ ] _____
- [ ] _____

Butcher/Deli
- [ ] _____
- [ ] _____
- [ ] _____
- [ ] _____
- [ ] _____
- [ ] _____
- [ ] _____
- [ ] _____
- [ ] _____

Italian/Mexican
- [ ] _____
- [ ] _____
- [ ] _____
- [ ] _____
- [ ] _____
- [ ] _____
- [ ] _____
- [ ] _____
- [ ] _____

Snacks
- [ ] _____
- [ ] _____
- [ ] _____
- [ ] _____
- [ ] _____
- [ ] _____
- [ ] _____
- [ ] _____
- [ ] _____

Bakery
- [ ] _____
- [ ] _____
- [ ] _____
- [ ] _____
- [ ] _____
- [ ] _____
- [ ] _____
- [ ] _____
- [ ] _____

Baking/Spices
- [ ] _____
- [ ] _____
- [ ] _____
- [ ] _____
- [ ] _____
- [ ] _____
- [ ] _____
- [ ] _____
- [ ] _____

Beverages
- [ ] _____
- [ ] _____
- [ ] _____
- [ ] _____
- [ ] _____
- [ ] _____

Home Care
- [ ] _____
- [ ] _____
- [ ] _____

Breakfast
- [ ] _____
- [ ] _____
- [ ] _____
- [ ] _____
- [ ] _____
- [ ] _____
- [ ] _____
- [ ] _____
- [ ] _____

Soup/Canned
- [ ] _____
- [ ] _____
- [ ] _____
- [ ] _____
- [ ] _____
- [ ] _____
- [ ] _____
- [ ] _____
- [ ] _____

Other
- [ ] _____
- [ ] _____
- [ ] _____
- [ ] _____
- [ ] _____
- [ ] _____

RECIPES

The following sections have recipes for all of the meals suggested in this book. I hope you find them helpful! Some of the more common meals are not included in this book.

SNACKS, SALADS & SIDES

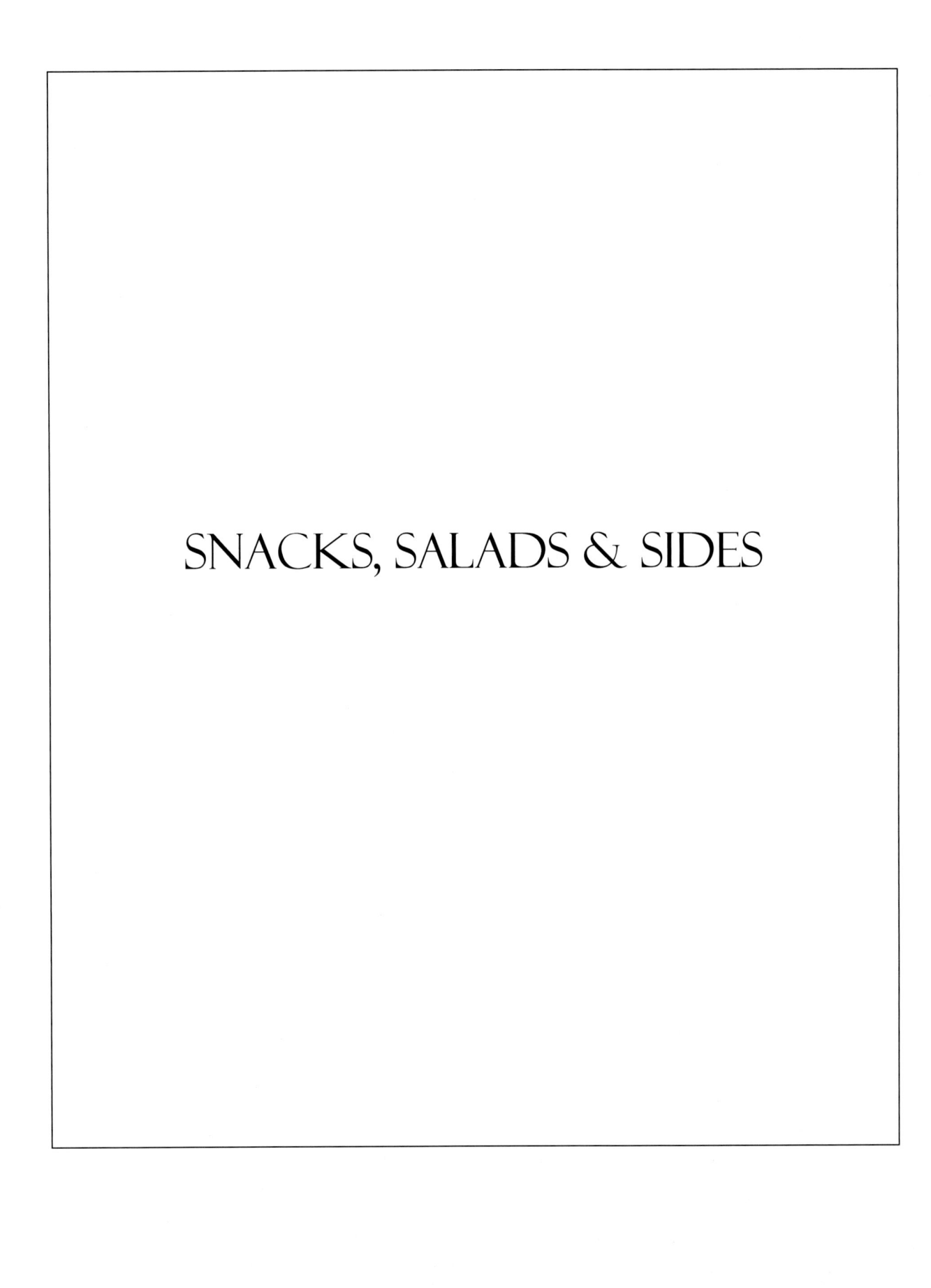

HEALTHY SNACK IDEAS

Fruit - Honey Crisp Apples - Pears - Kiwi - Grapes - Bananas - Oranges - Plums - Mango - Strawberries	**Veggies:** (optional: serve with ranch dip or dill dip recipes) - Cucumber slices - Carrots - Bell Peppers - Cherry or Grape Tomatoes - Broccoli - Snap peas - Radishes - Cauliflower - Edamame - Peaches - Blueberries - Celery (optional: serve with peanut butter)
Dry Snacks: (Tip: Buy dry snacks in bulk, then store in snack sized baggies. This helps the snacks last longer, and keeps them fresh!) - Pretzels - Goldfish - Granola Bars - Trail Mix - Chex Mix - Dry Cereals - Yogurt Covered Raisins - Fruit Leathers - Nuts & Seeds - Crackers - Popcorn	**Other Snacks:** - String Cheese - Yogurt - Pickles - Hard boiled eggs

CINNAMON TORTILLA CHIPS

Prep Time: 15 min. Cook Time: 15 min.	
10 (10 inch) flour tortillas Butter flavored cooking spray *(Can spray with water, but not as yummy!)* ½ c. sugar 2 Tbsp. ground cinnamon	1. Preheat oven to 350°F. 2. Combine cinnamon and sugar together in a small bowl and set aside. 3. Coat one side of each flour tortilla with butter flavored cooking spray. Cut into wedges and arrange in a single layer on a large baking sheet. Sprinkle wedges generously with cinnamon sugar mixture. 4. Bake for approx. 8 to 10 minutes or until chips are golden and crispy. Repeat with any remaining tortilla wedges. Allow to cool approximately 15 minutes. 5. Serve with chilled fruit salsa *(See recipe in this book.)*

EDIBLE CHRISTMAS TREES

Prep Time: 15 min.	
Sugar cones (one per child) Green frosting Various sprinkles for decorating: Red Hot candies, mini-M&Ms, sprinkles, etc. Butter knife to spread frosting	1. Spread green frosting all over outside of cone. 2. Roll in sprinkles 3. Push on red-hot candies or mini-M&Ms for ornaments

FRUIT SALSA

Prep Time: 15 min.	
2 kiwis, peeled and diced 2 apples – peeled, cored and diced 8 oz. raspberries, diced 1 lb. strawberries, diced ½ cantaloupe diced 1 Tbsp. white sugar *(Can be omitted)* 1 Tbsp. brown sugar *(Can substitute with sucanat)* 3 Tbsp. fruit preserves, any flavor works fine! I like Strawberry or apricot preserves. *Note: You can use any fruit you have on hand for this, just try to go for a variety of colors.*	Dice all ingredients finely and mix in a bowl. Let set in the refrigerator for at least 10 minutes prior to serving. Serve with Cinnamon Tortilla chips *(See recipe included in this book.)*

HOMEMADE GRANOLA BARS

Prep Time: 5 min. Cook Time: 35 min.	
2 c. rolled oats ¾ c. packed brown sugar ¾ tsp. ground cinnamon 1 c. whole wheat flour ¼ c. white chocolate chips *(Optional: any Dried Fruit, Raisins, Craisins, Nuts, Chocolate Chips, Coconut Flakes, have fun with this!)* ¾ tsp. salt ½ c. honey 1 egg, beaten ½ c. coconut oil *(Melted! I microwave about 30 seconds until liquid, this makes it MUCH easier to work with!)* 2 tsp. vanilla extract	1. Preheat oven to 350°F. 2. Grease a 9×13 baking dish. 3. Mix together dry ingredients, then make a well in the center and add the honey, beaten egg, melted coconut oil, and vanilla extract. Mix well. Pat the mixture evenly into the baking dish. 4. Bake for 30-35 minutes or until the edges are beginning to turn golden. 5. Cool for 5 minutes and then cut into bars and remove from dish WHILE STILL WARM. 6. Store in an air tight container.

ORANGE, WALNUT, CRAISIN SALAD

Prep Time: 5 min.	
Spinach leaves (or lettuce of your choice), ½ c. chopped mandarin orange slices (or regular oranges sliced), ¼ c. chopped walnuts ½ diced apple ¼ c. craisins	Place all ingredients in a bowl and toss well. Drizzle with a balsamic vinegar dressing.

SOFT PRETZELS

Prep Time: 20 min. **Cook Time:** 5 min.

Pretzels:
1 ¼ c. warm water
1 Tbsp. yeast
¼ c. brown sugar (Can substitute sucanat)
3 ½ – 4 c. whole wheat flour (Can substitute 2 c. bread flour + 2 c. regular flour)
Melted butter to rub on baked pretzels.
Coarse Salt

Dipping Solution:
¼ c. baking soda
2 ½ c. very hot water

1. Preheat oven to 500°F.
2. Dissolve yeast in warm water.
3. Add sugar, stir to dissolve, THEN add flour and mix until combined well. Do not over knead or dough will be tough.
4. Cut dough into 9 even chunks then roll into ropes and shape into pretzels, or whatever you children come up with.
5. Prepare dipping solution: Stir baking soda into hot water until dissolved, and then using a slotted spoon dip formed pretzels into the solution for a couple seconds each and place onto greased baking sheet.
6. Bake for 4-5 minutes or until pretzels are golden on top.
7. Either brush butter on warm pretzels, or melt it and dip the pretzels in the butter to coat. Sprinkle as desired with coarse salt. *(Can also spray with water instead of butter to make topping stick)*

Variations:

Cinnamon Sugar: Add 1, 4 tsp. to dough and then after baking, dip in butter and sprinkle with cinnamon sugar instead of salt.

Pizza: Top with garlic salt and parmesan cheese then dip in marinara sauce.

PEPPERMINT BARK

Prep, Cook Time: approx. 45 min.	
24 oz. white chocolate chips 24 oz. semisweet chocolate chips 1 tsp. peppermint extract 1 package Bob's Candy Canes Cookie Sheet lined Aluminum foil Cooking spray	1. Preheat oven to 250°F. 2. Line a cookie sheet with aluminum foil and spray with cooking spray. 3. Pour the semisweet chocolate chips onto the foil and spread them around evenly. Bake for a couple of minutes until they look barely melted. Then take the pan out of the oven and spread the chips around with a spatula. Put the pan in the refrigerator to cool and harden for about 30 minutes. 4. Place the candy canes on a cookie sheet under a dishtowel and crush them with a rolling pin. Sort the larger candy cane pieces from the candy cane dust and set aside. 5. Melt the white chocolate chips in a double boiler, stirring constantly. (You can also melt them in the microwaveable bowl for about 5 minutes, stirring half way in between.) 6. Stir in 1 tsp. of peppermint extract and the candy cane dust. Mix until smooth. 7. Spread white chocolate mix over the top of your COOLED semisweet chocolate layer. 8. Sprinkle top with candy cane pieces and press them down lightly so that they stick. 9. Refrigerate for several hours until firm, then break the bark into chunks. 10. Store in an airtight container in the fridge. Remove from fridge about 5 minutes before serving so no one breaks a tooth!

PIZZELLE COOKIES

Prep Time: 20 min. Cook Time: approx. 30 sec.-1min. per cookie	
6 eggs, beaten 1 ½ c. sugar 2 tsp. vanilla 2 sticks MARGARINE softened (Do not use butter!) 3 ½ c. flour (sifted 3 times) 2 tsp. baking powder Pizzelle Iron Flour Sifter Optional: Powdered Sugar	1. Beat eggs slowly and add sugar. Continue beating sugar and egg mixture until smooth. 2. Slowly beat in cooled but softened margarine and vanilla. 3. Sift flour and baking soda together at least three times, then mix into batter. 4. Drop approximately 1 Tbsp. of batter onto the Pizzelle Iron and bake until the light turns green, or pizzelles are a nice light golden color. 5. Optional: Sprinkle with powdered sugar and enjoy!

WHITE CHOCOLATE POPCORN

Prep Time: 10 min. **Cook Time:** approx. 3-5 min.	
1 large bag microwaveable butter flavor popcorn 2 c. mini marshmallows ½ c. roasted salted cashew pieces ½ c. dried cranberries 1 c. white chocolate chips LARGE microwave safe bowl Wax paper	1. Line a cookie sheet with waxed paper and set aside. 2. Pop 1 bag of popcorn and pour half of the hot popcorn into a large microwave-safe bowl. Top it with the marshmallows, cashews, and dried cranberries. Then top it with the rest of the hot popcorn and toss everything together. 3. Spread the popcorn mixture out on a sheet of wax paper. 4. Melt the white chocolate in the microwave for about 30 seconds on high, stir to smooth. If the chocolate is too thick, put the bowl in the microwave for 10 second increments until melted. 5. Drizzle the white chocolate over the popcorn until everything is nicely coated. 6. Cool completely, then gently break up the popcorn and put in cute little popcorn bowls for the family!

BREAKFAST

KID FRIENDLY GREEN SMOOTHIES

Prep Time: 5 min.	
2 c. Fresh spinach leaves 2 c. water 3 c. combination of frozen mango & pineapple chunks 1 banana, peeled Optional: 1, 2 lemon	1. Add water and spinach leaves to blender and blend on high until leaves are well pureed. 2. Add mango, pineapple, banana, and lemon. Blend well. 3. Serve immediately. *Tip*: Blend the greens first, before adding any fruit. They will blend much better if done first.

ORANGE SMOOTHIE

Prep Time: 5 min.	
2 c. orange juice ½ c. milk 8 Ice cubes 2 Tbsp. powdered sugar	Place all ingredients in a blender and blend until smooth! Serve with your favorite breakfast, or have as a mid-day snack!

YOGURT PARFAIT

Prep Time: 5 min.	
½ c. vanilla yogurt ¼ c. blueberries ¼ c. strawberries 1 Tbsp. granola Optional: Sprinkle top with light brown sugar	Place all ingredients in a bowl and serve! (Of course you can substitute the fruit for anything you prefer.)

PANCAKES

Prep Time: 10 min. **Cook Time:** 3-5min. each	
1 ¼ c. whole wheat flour 1 Tbsp. sugar (Can substitute 1 Tbsp. honey) 2 tsp. baking powder 1 c. milk 2 Tbsp. lemon juice 1 egg, beaten *Optional*: 1, 4 c your favorite ingredient. Some ideas we like: white chocolate chips, blueberries, strawberries.	Mix all ingredients in a bowl and cook on flat skillet until browned on both sides. Top with a pat of butter and Agave Nectar. *Makes about 14 small pancakes.*

DIPS

CREAMY DILL DIP RECIPE

Prep Time: 5 min. Chill Time: 45 mins.	
1 c. (8 oz.) sour cream (optional: low fat) 1 c. mayonnaise (optional: low fat) 1 Tbsp. minced fresh parsley 1 Tbsp. dill weed ¾ tsp. seasoned salt	Mix all ingredients in a bowl. Cover and refrigerate for about 30-45 min. or until chilled. Serve with your favorite veggies!

CREAMY RANCH DIP RECIPE

Prep Time: 5 min. Chill Time: 45 mins.	
½ c. (8 oz.) low fat sour cream ½ c. low fat mayonnaise ½ tsp. dried or fresh chives ½ tsp. dried parsley ½ tsp. dried dill weed ¼ tsp. garlic powder ¼ tsp. onion powder 1/8 tsp. salt 1/8 tsp. black pepper (or to taste) (optional: If you have buttermilk on hand substitute the sour cream for ½ c. buttermilk and then add ¼ c. sour cream! It's delicious!)	Mix all ingredients in a bowl. Cover and refrigerate for about 30-45 min. or until chilled. Serve with your favorite veggies or as a salad dressing!

MAIN DISHES

BBQ RIBS

Prep Time: 15 min. Cook Time: 1 hour, 10 mins.	
3-4 lbs. Baby Back or Spare Ribs 32 oz. Pineapple Juice 1 c. soy sauce 1 c. sugar ½ c. + 1 Tbsp. of white vinegar Corn Starch to thicken (Start with 4 Tbsp.) Aluminum foil	**Sauce:** Heat sauce in sauce pan until slightly bubbling. Remove from heat once thickened and cool. **Ribs:** Sprinkle salt, pepper to taste on ribs. Preheat oven to 375°F. Bake ribs covered for approximately 40 minutes, turn over and bake another 25 minutes uncovered. Brush sauce on top side of ribs and cook about 5 minutes longer.

BBQ PULLED CHICKEN

Prep Time: 15 min. Cook Time: 1 hour, 10 mins.	
4 boneless, skinless chicken breasts ¼ c. Italian dressing (Any kind will work) ¼ c. brown sugar 1 c. BBQ sauce (Any kind) Salt/Pepper to taste Slow cooker	Mix dressing, brown sugar, and BBQ sauce in a bowl and set aside. Place raw (thawed) chicken into your slow cooker and set to low. Pour sauce mixture over chicken and let cook on low for about 5-6 hours or until done. Once done, pull chicken apart with a fork, shredding it. Serving suggestions: Serve on hamburger buns, or alone, with chips, pasta salad, green salad, coleslaw, corn, fruit, or your favorite veggie to complete the meal!

BREADED CHICKEN

Prep Time: 10 min. Cook Time: 45 min.	
6 boneless, skinless chicken thighs or breasts ½ c. seasoned bread crumbs ¼ c. shredded parmesan cheese 1 egg (beaten) ½ c. milk cooking spray olive oil	1. Preheat oven to 350°F and spray a 9×13 pan with cooking oil. 2. Mix breadcrumbs & shredded parmesan cheese in shallow bowl. 3. Beat egg and milk together in separate shallow bowl. 4. Dip each chicken breast into egg mixture then coat with bread crumbs and place into 9×13 pan. 5. Drizzle breaded chicken breasts with olive oil and bake uncovered for approx. 45 minutes or until golden brown.

BEEF BRISKET

Prep Time: 10 min. Cook Time: 6 hours, 15 min.	
1 beef brisket (approx. 3lbs) Garlic Salt Black Pepper 2 Tbps. Beef Bouillon Granules Favorite BBQ Sauce (optional) Aluminum foil	1. Preheat oven to 475°F. 2. Place brisket in roasting pan and coat generously with garlic salt and crushed black pepper. 3. Sprinkle 2 T of Beef Bouillon granules over the top of the brisket. 4. Cook uncovered for about 15 minutes. 5. Cover with foil and reduce heat to 225 °F. Cook for approx. 6 hours or until done. 6. Remove from oven and let set about 10 minutes before slicing to keep meat moist. 7. Optional: Serve with BBQ sauce.

BEEF & BEAN BURRITOS

Prep Time: 20 min. Cook Time: 45 min.	
10-12 flour tortillas 1 lb. ground beef 1 can black beans, drained ½ medium onion, finely diced 1 16oz. can Hatch's Green Enchilada Sauce Monterrey, Colby cheese, shredded Optional garnish: guacamole, sour cream, lettuce, tomato	1. Preheat oven to 350°F. 2. In Skillet, sauté onions and beef until done. 3. Add black beans to meat and stir until warmed, just a few minutes. 4. Pour a small amount of the green enchilada sauce on the bottom of a 9×13 baking dish. 5. Fill tortillas with beef mixture, wrap and add to pan. 6. Once pan is full, top burritos with green enchilada sauce and sprinkle with cheese. 7. Bake for about 45 minutes until warm and bubbly. Optional: Serve with Spanish rice, beans, guacamole, sour cream, shredded lettuce, diced tomatoes!

BEEF & BROCCOLI (MONGOLIAN)

Prep Time: 15 min. **Cook Time:** approx. 25 mins.

2 Tbsp Vegetable oil 1 tsp Ginger, minced *(I used ground ginger and it was fine)* 2 Tbsp Garlic, chopped 1/2 c. Soy sauce 1 c. Dark brown sugar 1/2 c. Vegetable oil 1 lb. Flank steak or sirloin sliced thinly 1/4 c. Cornstarch 3 Green onions sliced or 2 Cups Broccoli steamed	1. Heat 2 tbsp vegetable oil in skillet over medium high heat until hot. Add ginger and garlic and let sizzle for 30 seconds, then add soy sauce. Gradually add the brown sugar and let it dissolve while stirring. Let the sauce come to a boil, then simmer for 2-3 minutes. Remove from heat and set aside. 2. Cut the flank steak into thin strips against the grain. *(Tip: Meat is easier to slice when it's partially frozen. It will thaw quickly after sliced too!)* Place meat and corn starch in a bag and shake to coat the meat. Let meat sit for 10 minutes, so the cornstarch sticks to the meat. 3. Put 1/2 c. vegetable oil in a wok/ skillet and heat on medium-high until hot. Add the meat to the wok and brown for about 4-5 minutes. Remove the meat from the pan with a slotted spoon and place on paper towels to drain. 4. Clean the pan out and return meat to pan and cook on high for about 2 more minutes. Add the sauce to the pan and cook for another minute. Add the green onions or broccoli and cook for 1 minute longer. 5. Remove from heat and serve with rice.

BEEF STROGANOFF

Prep Time: 10 min. Cook Time: 35 min.	
1 pkg. Wide egg noodles 1 jar brown gravy (or make your own!) 1 can mushroom pieces (or 1 c. chopped mushrooms 1 sm. yellow onion, diced 1 Tbsp. butter	1. Cook egg noodles according to directions on package and drain. Set aside. 2. In sauté pan melt butter, sauté onions until soft. 3. Add gravy and mushrooms to sauté pan and cook until mushrooms are soft. 4. Serve sauce mixture over noodles. Optional: Serve with your favorite veggie or side salad

BREADED CAULIFLOWER

Prep Time: 5 min. Cook Time: approx. 10-15 min.	
1 head of cauliflower, cut into approx. 1" chunks (Can sub. Frozen package) 2 Tbsp. butter ½ c. bread crumbs Salt/pepper	1. Heat butter in sauté pan and add cauliflower. 2. Stir to coat with butter, then sprinkle bread crumbs over the top of the cauliflower. 3. Stir occasionally until cauliflower is cooked through. 4. Salt/pepper as desired.

CORN AND CHEESE CHOWDER

Prep Time: 15 min. **Cook Time:** approx. 25 min.	
4 Tbsp. butter (1/2 stick) 1/2 sweet onion, diced 3 slices bacon, diced 1 red bell pepper, diced 1 can corn, drained (Can also use creamed corn) 1/4 c. All-purpose flour 3 c. chicken broth 2 c. half-and-half 2 c. shredded Monterey Jack cheese 1/4 c. green onion, sliced Optional: Bread Bowls (1 per person)	1. In large pot, melt butter over medium-high heat. Cook onions for a few minutes, then add in bacon and diced bell peppers. Cook until soft. Add in corn and simmer a couple more minutes. 2. Sprinkle flour over mixture, and stir. Add in broth and simmer for 3-4 minutes. 3. Reduce heat to low, then stir in half-and-half, cover to thicken and simmer for about 15 minutes. 4. Stir in cheese and green onion, then salt and pepper to taste. Optional: Serve in bread bowls, top with a little extra cheese and green onion if desired.

CREAMY CHICKEN BURRITOS

Prep Time: 15 min. **Cook Time:** 45 min.	
2-4 boneless chicken thighs ¼ yellow onion diced 1 clove garlic, minced 1 tsp. each: oregano, basil, cumin Sm. Can diced peeled green chilies 1 can cream of chicken soup 2 c. Instant rice (prepared) 2 heaping Tbsp. Sour Cream 1 large can Hatch Green Enchilada Sauce 1 c. Shredded Monterrey, Colby cheese Olive oil for cooking *(about 1-2 Tbsp.)* Flour Tortillas Optional: garnish with guacamole, sour cream, shredded lettuce, diced tomatoes	1. Drizzle olive oil in pan and Sauté chicken, onion, garlic, spices and chopped chili until chicken is cooked through. Once chicken is cooked, remove from pan and shred or slice into small cubes. 2. Prepare 2 cups instant rice. 3. In medium bowl, mix together chicken mixture, prepared rice, 1, 2 cup shredded cheese, 2 heaping Tbsp. sour cream and 1 can cream of chicken soup. 4. Drizzle 9×13 pan with green chili enchilada sauce. 5. Fill tortillas with mixture, wrap into burritos and place in 9×13 pan. 6. Top finished burritos with remaining green chili sauce and sprinkle more shredded cheese on top. 7. Bake uncovered for 45 minutes or until warm and bubbly.

CALZONES

Prep Time: 6 hrs. Cook Time: 30 min.	
1 loaf Rhode's frozen bread dough (can sub. Pillsbury pizza dough.) 1 Jar of your favorite Marinara Sauce Mozzarella Cheese, shredded Toppings: Canadian Bacon, Pepperoni, Mushrooms, Browned Sausage, Black Olives, Green Bell Peppers, Onions, etc.	1. Preheat oven to 350°F. 2. Place frozen dough in greased bowl and cover with a towel or greased plastic wrap. Let rise 6-7 hours or until doubled. 3. Divide dough into equal parts for desired amount of calzones. Roll out prepared dough onto a floured surface about 1, 4 – 1, 8 inch thick. 4. Fill one half of the dough with toppings of your choice, add cheese and sauce. 5. Fold over top layer of dough and pinch around edges to seal well. 6. Place completed calzone on greased or wax paper lined baking sheet. 7. Bake approx. 30 minutes or until crust is golden brown on top. Serve with salad and extra bowl of marinara sauce for dipping! Yum! **Tip:** Label calzones with a toothpick and a piece of wax paper with your initials on it so they don't get mixed up!

CHICKEN LETTUCE WRAPS

Prep Time: 5 min. **Cook Time:** approx. 15 min.	
4-6 Chicken Thighs or ground beef (minced, I use my Pampered Chef Chopper) 1/4 c. julienned carrots (In salad section of produce, or slice your own!) 2 Tbsp. fresh minced ginger 1/4 c. low sodium Soy Sauce 1 Tbsp. rice vinegar 1/4 tsp. sesame oil 1/8 tsp. crushed red pepper 1/2 c. thinly sliced green onion 1/4 c. chopped fresh cilantro ice burg lettuce leaves	1. Heat large - skillet over medium heat until hot. 2. Add meat, carrots and ginger. Sauté until meat is cooked. Drain if necessary, and return meat mixture to pan. 3. Stir in soy sauce, vinegar, sesame oil and red pepper. Cook about 1 minute, remove from heat and stir in green onions and cilantro. 4. Serve in lettuce leaves.

COCONUT CHICKEN

Prep Time: 15 min. **Cook Time:** 45 min.

4-6 chicken thighs 1/3 c. dry plain breadcrumbs 1/3 c. flaked coconut ¼ c. butter, melted (can substitute olive oil) Salt & Pepper (to taste) Cooking Spray Optional: aluminum foil	1. Season chicken with salt & pepper to taste. 2. In a separate plate mix breadcrumbs and coconut together. 3. Roll chicken thighs in breadcrumb mixture 1 at a time to coat well. 4. Place coated chicken in lightly sprayed baking dish and drizzle with olive oil. 5. Bake for 45-55 minutes until chicken is done.

CROCKPOT ROTISSERIE CHICKEN

Prep Time: 5 min. **Cook Time:** 4-6 hours

1 whole roasting chicken Olive oil Salt Garlic salt Onion salt Black pepper Aluminum foil	1. Make 4-5 loose balls of foil and place in the bottom of your crockpot. 2. Clean chicken inside and out, then rub chicken all over with olive oil. 3. Sprinkle chicken with salt, garlic salt, onion salt, and black pepper, and rub into skin well. 4. Place chicken back side down in crockpot on top of foil balls. 5. Cook on high for 4-6 hours or until chicken is done. Note: The foil balls will collect any fat from the chicken cooking.

CHICKEN PARMESAN

Prep Time: 10 min. Cook Time: approx. 25 min.	
1/3 c. Italian style bread crumbs 6 oz. tomato paste 1 14.5 oz. can diced tomatoes with garlic 4 oz. fettuccine 4 boneless, skinless chicken breasts 1 c. milk 1 Tbsp. olive oil ¼ c. parmesan cheese, grated	1. Cook pasta according to package directions and drain. 2. Dip chicken in milk, then coat with bread crumbs. 3. Cook chicken in hot oil in large skillet over medium heat 10 minutes or until done, and browned on both sides. Remove chicken and keep warm. 4. Stir un-drained tomatoes, tomato paste and 1, 2 c. water into skillet. Bring to boil; reduce heat and simmer 3 minutes or until heated through. 5. Serve sauce over chicken and fettuccine. Sprinkle with cheese.

CHICKEN OR STEAK KABOBS

Prep Time: 15 min. Cook Time: approx. 10-15 min.	
1-2 chicken breasts, cubed (OR 1-2 steaks cubed.) 1 bell pepper, cut in 1" cubes 1 yellow onion, cut in 1" cubes 1 pkg. whole mushrooms 1 pkg. cherry tomatoes Salt/pepper to taste BBQ Skewers Optional: BBQ Sauce	5. Layer all ingredients onto BBQ skewers and season as desired. Salt/pepper, and BBQ sauce make a great seasoning mix! 6. Grill on medium heat until chicken is cooked through. Serve with seasonal fruit or side salad.

CHICKEN STIR-FRY

Prep Time: 15 min. Cook Time: 25 min.	
6 chicken thighs (Diced) 1 bottle Stir-Fry Sauce (Asian Isle) 2 Tbsp. Asian Stir-Fry Seasoning (Asian Isle) 1 c. Frozen edamame (shelled) 1 c. julienne carrots (produce section) 1 c. broccoli (optional) Optional: 6 c. cooked White Rice	1. Heat 1 tsp. vegetable oil in sauté pan. 2. Add veggies into pan. Cook about 3-5 minutes until veggies are slightly tender. 3. Place stir-fry sauce, Asian Stir-Fry Seasoning, and diced chicken thighs in skillet and sauté about 20 minutes or until chicken is done. 4. Serve over rice.

ENCHILADA CASSEROLE

Prep Time: 5 min. Cook Time: 40 min.	
12 corn tortillas (the soft kind) 2 lbs. of hamburger browned 1 can Cream of Chicken Soup 1 small can chopped green chili 1 small can Pet Evaporated Milk 1 ½ cans (14 oz.) Red Enchilada Sauce Shredded Monterrey Jack Cheese Aluminum foil	1. Preheat oven to 350°F 2. Brown hamburger and drain. Add soup, chili's, enchilada sauce and milk; Simmer for 10 minutes. Line bottom of 13x9 pan with 1 layer of tortillas. Add 1, 3 meat mixture, top with cheese. Repeat Layers until pan is full. Top with cheese and extra enchilada sauce. 3. Cover and bake for 25 to 30 min. 4. Serve with lettuce, sour cream, guacamole, & diced tomatoes, and Spanish rice! *Tip*: This makes a great freezer meal, simply prepare as directed above but don't bake it. Cover casserole dish well and freeze. When you're ready to eat them, thaw overnight in refrigerator.

CHICKEN OR STEAK FAJITAS

Prep Time: 15 min. **Cook Time:** 10-12 min.

6 chicken thighs (or 1 lb. of Sirloin Steak), cut into thin slices 1 green bell pepper sliced 1 red bell pepper sliced ½ medium onion sliced ¼ c. olive oil ¼ c. canola oil 1 Tbsp. oregano 1 Tbsp. basil 1 Tbsp. parsley 1 tsp. garlic salt 1 tsp. onion salt Tortillas *Optional*: guacamole, sour cream, shredded lettuce, diced tomatoes *Tip:* If you have time, make this earlier in the day, and place in a Ziploc baggie to marinate until ready to cook!	1. Turn oven to broil. 2. Place meat and veggies onto a cookie sheet, spreading out evenly. 3. Pour all oils and spices on top of the meat and mix well with hands. *(If I'm doing meat and chicken, I put them on separate cookie sheets.)* 4. Broil fajitas on high for about 5-6 minutes, flip meat and broil another 5-6 minutes until done. 5. Serve on tortillas with guacamole, sour cream, shredded lettuce, diced tomatoes, rice, beans, salsa, etc. **Note:** This is a great freezer meal, just slice the raw meat and put in a Gallon Ziploc baggie along with the oils and spices. In a separate bag put the sliced veggies. Freeze the bags and then thaw overnight. Prepare as directed above.

FRENCH DIP

Prep Time: 5 min. Cook Time: 10 min.	
1 lb. sliced deli roast beef Provolone Cheese slices Hoagie rolls 1 10.5 oz. can beef consommé 1 c. water Salt/pepper to taste	1. Pre-heat oven to 350°F 2. Heat beef consommé and water in medium sauce pan over medium-high heat. 3. Place roast beef slices in sauce for about 2 minutes or until warmed. 4. Arrange hoagies on a cookie sheet and add beef on to each hoagie. Place 2 slices of cheese on each one. 5. Bake in pre-heated oven for about 5 minutes or until the cheese melts. 6. Ladle remaining broth into small bowls for dipping, and serve with the sandwiches.

FRIED RICE

Prep Time: 5 min. Cook Time: approx. 15 min.	
2 c. cooked instant white rice 1 sm. bag frozen peas and carrots 1 egg 2 Tbsp. butter Salt/pepper to taste Splash of Soy Sauce	5. Cook rice according to package directions. Set aside. 6. In saute pan, melt butter and add 1 egg, stir well, and cook until scrambled. 7. Add peas/carrots to eggs and cook until heated. 8. Add rice, and a splash of soy sauce for flavor. 9. Salt and pepper to taste.

GREEN CHILI

Prep Time: 10 min. **Cook Time:** 55 min.	
2 Tbsp. vegetable oil 1 ½ lbs. cubed pork stew meat *(may substitute with chicken)* 2 Tbsp. all-purpose flour 1 (4.5 oz.) can diced green Chile peppers, drained ½ (3.5 oz.) can chopped jalapeno peppers ½ medium onion, chopped 5 Tbsp. tomato sauce 3 ½ c. water onion salt to taste garlic salt to taste salt and black pepper to taste	1. Heat oil in a large pot over medium-high heat. Stir in cubed pork, and cook until nicely browned and cooked through, about 15 minutes. Remove skillet from heat, and drain fat. 2. Sprinkle flour over pork. With a wooden spoon, stir pork to coat, scraping the bottom of the pot to loosen browned bits. Add chile peppers, jalapenos, and onions and stir. 3. Add tomato sauce and water. Season to taste with onion salt, garlic salt, and salt and pepper. 4. Return pot to medium heat. Bring to a simmer, cover, and cook 30 minutes, stirring occasionally. Remove cover, and cook 10 minutes more. Serve with homemade tortillas. *(See recipe in this book.)*

HAM AND WHITE BEAN SOUP

Prep Time: 10 min. **Cook Time:** approx. 6 hours	
Leftover ham bone (with ham on it) 16 oz. bag of northern white beans ½ sweet onion finely diced Optional: diced carrot and celery (or any other veggie you like in your soup) Optional: 1 Tbsp. Apple Cider Vinegar	1. Place ham bone and beans into a stockpot and cover with water. Simmer all day on low heat. 2. Add your onions and other veggies about 1 hour prior to eating so they cook until soft. 3. If you want a little fresh kick to your soup add 1 Tbsp. of apple cider vinegar right at the very end.

HOMEMADE PIZZA

Prep Time: 15 min. Cook Time: 20 mins.	
7 ½ c. flour 1 Tbsp. salt 1 Tbsp. yeast 3 c. warm water 1 jar Pizza sauce Shredded mozzarella cheese Your favorite pizza toppings	1. Preheat oven to 425°F. 2. In large bowl mix together yeast, & warm water, then add flour & salt. Finally add in flour slowly. Knead together for 6-10 minutes until dough is smooth. I use a Bosch Mixer to knead my dough, but this is super easy to hand knead. 3. Divide dough into 2 even pieces and roll into circle shape. Place dough onto a greased cookie sheet. 4. Bake dough at 425°F for 5-8 minutes and remove from oven and add sauce, cheese and other desired toppings. Continue baking for another 15-18 minutes until crust is golden and cheese is melted.

HOMEMADE FLOUR TORTILLAS

Prep Time: 40 min. Cook Time: 20 min.	
2 c. whole wheat flour (Can substitute regular flour) ½ tsp salt ¼ c. oil 2/3 c. warm water	1. Mix ingredients together by hand, let sit covered 30 minutes. 2. Roll into 12 balls and press with tortilla press or roll out with rolling pin. 3. Cook both sides on a warm skillet until lightly browned.

HOT TACO SOUP

Prep Time: 5 min. **Cook Time:** 40 min.	
1 ½ lbs. extra lean ground beef 1 medium Onion, chopped 1 – 17 oz. can diced tomatoes with juice 2 – 14 oz. cans kidney beans 1 – 14 oz. can of corn w, juice 1 package Taco Seasoning 1 tsp. garlic powder 1 tsp. chili powder 1 c. chicken broth Optional garnish: shredded cheddar cheese, diced avocado, sour cream, sliced green onion, Fritos	1. In large stockpot, brown ground beef and onion. 2. Drain grease, add all remaining ingredients. Simmer for at least 30 minutes. 3. Serve in individual bowls and garnish as desired! Note: Make your own taco seasoning! *See recipe included in this book.*

ITALIAN BEEF POT-ROAST

Prep Time: 5 min. **Cook Time:** 6 hours	
1 Beef Chuck Roast (size to your family's needs, can also use chicken thighs) 1 packet Good Seasonings Italian dressing (Dry mix) 1 can inexpensive beer *(I don't typically use alcohol in my cooking, however this really was worth it and there was no alcohol taste left over, just super tender beef.)*	1. Place roast in crockpot on high, sprinkle dry dressing mix on top of roast and cover with 1 can of beer. 2. Cook in crockpot 6 hours on high.

LASAGNA ROLL-UPS

Prep Time: 10 min. **Cook Time:** 45 min.	
6-12 Lasagna sheets (1-2 per person) 1 c. browned ground beef (or ground turkey) ½ tsp. each: garlic salt and onion salt 1 c. frozen chopped spinach, thawed & drained. ½ c. low-fat Ricotta cheese ½ c. mozzarella cheese, shredded ¼ c. Parmesan cheese, grated 1 Tbsp. each: dried basil, oregano, parsley 1 jar spaghetti sauce Optional: 1 c. parmesan sprinkled on top Aluminum foil	1. Preheat oven to 375°F. Spray 9x13 baking dish with non-stick cooking spray. Then pour 1 c. spaghetti sauce on the bottom of the dish and set aside. 2. In a large pot, bring water to a boil, and cook lasagna noodles according to package until done. 3. Meanwhile, in a medium skillet, cook ground beef, garlic salt, and onion salt until browned. Drain and set aside. 4. In a medium sized bowl, mix together spinach, ricotta, mozzarella, parmesan, basil, oregano, and parsley. Add meat to mixture and stir well. 5. Drain cooked noodles, and lay on a kitchen towel to dry. 6. In 9x13 casserole dish, spread a thin layer of spaghetti sauce. 7. Assemble the rolls by spreading some of the meat mixture over each noodle to cover most of the surface. Roll each one up, then place in the baking dish. 8. Once all rolls are completed, top them with remaining sauce, and sprinkle parmesan cheese on top. 9. Bake for approximately 30 minutes covered with foil, or until warmed through. Tip: Cook a few extra noodles then you'll need in case one breaks or tears.

MEATBALLS

Prep Time: 5 min. **Cook Time:** 40-50 min.	
1 lb. ground beef 1 egg ½ c. parmesan cheese ½ c. bread crumbs 1 Tbsp. each: Basil, Oregano, Parsley Salt/pepper to taste	1. Pre-heat oven to 350°F 2. Mix all ingredients in a bowl. 3. Form meatballs into golf ball sized balls. 4. Place on baking sheet and bake approx. 40 minutes or until done.

MEATLOAF

Prep Time: 10 min. **Cook Time:** 45 min.	
1-2 lbs. ground beef ¼ c. bread crumbs ¼ c. Parmesan cheese (either shredded or grated) 1 egg beaten 1 Tbsp. Parsley 1 Tbsp. Basil 1 Tbsp. Oregano ½ Tbsp. Garlic Salt ½ Tbsp. Onion Salt ¼ c. Ketchup	1. Preheat oven to 350°F 2. Mix all ingredients in a bowl, and pat into loaf shape. 3. Place meatloaf in loaf pan and bake for approximately 45 minutes. Tip: Mix ½ c. brown sugar and ½ c. ketchup together, then spread over top of meatloaf while cooking for a nice sauce.

PARSLEY POTATOES

Prep Time: 10 min. **Cook Time:** 20 min.	
Russet potatoes (1 per person) butter 1 Tbsp. parsley 1 tsp. garlic salt 1 tsp. onion salt	1. Fill large sauce pan with water and bring to boil. 2. Wash potatoes thoroughly, then dice into about 1" pieces and place in boiling water. Cook approximately 15 minutes or until tender. Drain water. 3. Meanwhile, melt approx. 4 Tbsp. of butter in sauté pan on low. Add garlic salt, onion salt and parsley. 4. Stir cooked potatoes into butter mixture until coated well and serve!

PENNE PASTA BAKE

Prep Time: 20 min. **Cook Time:** 40 min.	
1 - 15 oz. can tomato sauce 1 - 14.5 oz. can diced tomatoes with herbs 6 oz. tomato paste 12 oz. penne pasta 1 lb. ground beef 1 c. chopped onion 4 c. shredded mozzarella cheese	1. Preheat oven to 350°F 2. Cook pasta according to directions. 3. Cook meat and onion in large skillet over medium heat until browned. Stir in tomato sauce, diced tomatoes with juice, tomato paste, and ½ c. water. Simmer sauce approximately 10 minutes. 4. Layer half pasta, half sauce, and half cheese in a 13x9 backing dish. Repeat layer. Cover and bake for 20 minutes.

PINWHEELS

Prep Time: 10 min.	
Tortillas Spreadable cream cheese (You can also use mayonnaise and mustard in place of the cream cheese.) *Optional toppings:* Deli sliced ham Roast beef Turkey Sliced cucumber Avocado Sliced cheese Tomato Lettuce	1. Spread cream cheese on one side of your tortilla. 2. Top with your favorite ingredients. 3. Roll up the tortilla and slice into 1" sections and serve! Note: The pinwheels are a super fast and easy lunch or dinner idea! You can top them with virtually anything you like. We've even done PB&J pinwheels. Get creative and let your kids help make their own creations!

PORK ROAST

Prep Time: 10 min. **Cook Time:** 6-7 hours	
1 - 7 lb. Pork Shoulder (or butt) ¼ c. olive oil 2 Tbsp. garlic salt 2 Tbsp. onion salt 1 tsp. crushed black pepper 1 Tbsp. Parsley	4. Preheat oven to 275°F. 5. Place roast in roasting pan, and coat generously with olive oil 6. Sprinkle a good amount of remaining ingredients over roast and 'rub' in so that the roast has a good coating of spices. 7. Cook uncovered at 275°F for about 6 hours or until roast reads done using a meat thermometer. It should have a nice salty crust on the outside when it's finished, and your house will smell wonderful!

SCALLOP POTATOES

Prep Time: 5 min. **Cook Time:** 40 min.	
2-3 c. thinly sliced potatoes (Can sub. shredded frozen hash browns) 4 Tbsp. butter 1 ½ c. half-and-half ½ c. shredded cheddar cheese Salt/pepper to taste	5. Pre-heat oven to 350°F 6. In casserole dish, layer potatoes in bottom, and mix in shredded cheese. 7. Pour half-and-half over the top. 8. Place butter pats on top. 9. Salt/pepper to taste. 10. Bake uncovered for about 40 minutes or until potatoes are cooked through and cheese is melted.

SLOPPY JOES

Prep Time: 10 min. Cook Time: 40 min.	
1 lb. ground beef ½ c. finely diced onion ¼ c. finely diced green bell pepper ½ tsp. garlic powder 1 tsp. yellow mustard ¾ c. ketchup 1 Tbsp. brown sugar Salt and pepper to taste Hamburger buns	1. Brown ground beef, onion, and green bell pepper in a skillet over medium heat until browned, drain. 2. Stir in garlic powder, mustard, ketchup, brown sugar, salt, and pepper. 3. Reduce heat and simmer for about 30 minutes. Serve on a hamburger bun.

SPANISH RICE

Prep Time: 10 min. Cook Time: 20 min.	
¼ c. vegetable oil (enough to cover bottom of skillet) 1 c. long-grain white rice (can sub. Instant rice if you're in a hurry) ¼ c. tomato sauce 2 ½ c. water 2 Tbsp. Knorr chicken bouillon seasoning	1. In 12 inch or larger skillet, heat oil. Add rice, stirring often until golden brown then stir in tomato sauce. 2. Mix 2 1, 2 cups of water and Knorr seasoning together, and add to skillet. 3. Bring to a boil, reduce heat to low, cover and simmer about 20 minutes or until rice is tender and liquid has been absorbed. *(Do not mix while simmering or rice will become sticky.)* 4. Let it rest for about 5 minutes before serving.

SWEET AND SOUR PORK CHOPS

Prep Time: 10 min. **Cook Time:** 15 min.	
4-6 bone in pork chops ½ c. water ¼ c. cider vinegar ¼ c. packed brown sugar 2 Tbsp. soy sauce 1 Tbsp. Worcestershire sauce 1 Tbsp. corn starch 2 Tbsp. cold water Salt and pepper to taste	1. Season pork chops with salt and pepper. In skillet, cook pork over medium heat for 4-6 minutes on each side until lightly browned. Remove and keep warm. 2. To the skillet add water, vinegar, brown sugar, soy sauce, and Worcestershire sauce and mix well. 3. Combine cornstarch and 2 Tbsp. water until smooth, and add to skillet. Bring to a light boil and cook for 2 minutes or until thickened. 4. Return pork to the skillet, and coat with sauce. Simmer 4-5 minutes or until meat is fully cooked.

STUFFED SHELLS

Prep Time: 20 min. Cook Time: 45 min.	
1 box Jumbo pasta shells 1 lb. lean ground beef 1 clove garlic, minced 2 c. Mozzarella Cheese, shredded ½ c. seasoned bread crumbs 1 Tbsp. parsley flakes 1 egg, beaten ½ c. grated Parmesan Cheese ½ c. low-fat ricotta cheese 2 jars spaghetti sauce Aluminum foil	1. Preheat oven to 350°F. 2. Cook pasta shells according to directions, just until tender. 3. Meanwhile, brown beef and garlic in a skillet, drain. 4. Mix remaining ingredients in bowl and add beef mixture when done. 5. Line bottom of 9×13 pan with some of the sauce 6. Stuff shells and place in pan as you go. 7. Cover finished shells with sauce 8. Bake (covered w, foil) for 40 minutes, or until warmed through. 9. During last 10 minutes of cooking top with a handful of shredded mozzarella cheese until melted. Serve with: Garlic bread and salad

TACO SALAD

Prep Time: 10 min. Cook Time: 20 min.	
1 lb. browned ground beef or turkey 1 Tbsp. taco seasoning 2 Tbsp. water 1 can drained black beans 1 can drained chick peas 1 sm. can sliced black olives Lettuce of your choice (I used baby spinach leaves) 1 tomato, diced *Optional Garnish:* Salsa, 1 sliced green onion, shredded cheese, sour cream, Tortilla Strips (Found in the salad dressing isle of the grocery store)	1. Heat a large nonstick skillet over medium-high heat until hot. Add turkey, beef; cook 7 minutes or until browned, stirring to crumble. Drain if necessary and return to pan. Stir in taco seasoning and 2 Tbsp. water, cook another 1-2 minutes. 2. Add remaining ingredients except garnish to pan and stir just enough to mix. 3. Serve on plate of lettuce, and garnish as desired.

TACO SEASONING

Prep Time: 5 min.	
1 Tbsp. chili powder ¼ t. garlic powder ¼ t. onion powder ¼ t. crushed red pepper flakes ¼ t. oregano ½ t. paprika 1 ½ t. cumin 1 t. salt 1 t. black pepper	1. Mix all ingredients together in a bowl. 2. Store in air-tight container at room temp.

TATER-TOT CASSEROLE

Prep Time: 15 min. **Cook Time:** 45 min.	
1 can cream of mushroom soup 1 tsp. ketchup 1 tsp. Worcestershire sauce 1 lb. ground beef ½ diced onion chopped 1 bag frozen tater tots 1 ½ c. shredded Cheddar cheese Salt and pepper to taste Cooking Spray Optional: frozen peas	1. Preheat oven to 350°F 2. Brown ground beef and onion in sauté pan and drain grease, and salt and pepper to taste. Optional: add frozen peas to meat mixture 3. Add cream of mushroom soup, ketchup, and Worcestershire sauce to meat mixture and mix well. 4. Spray bottom of a 9×13 casserole dish and spread meat mixture evenly across bottom. 5. Arrange tater tots evenly over beef layer. 6. Sprinkle shredded cheddar cheese evenly over the top. 7. Bake for about 30 minutes or until cheese is bubbly.

TORTELLINI SOUP

Prep Time: 10 min. **Cook Time:** 45 min.	
6 links Sweet Italian Sausage 4 links German Sausage 2 cloves garlic chopped ½ yellow onion, chopped 2 Tbsp. olive oil 2 cans beef broth plus 2 cans water (fill broth cans with water after pouring in broth.) 1 - 16 oz. can petite diced tomatoes 1 ½ tsp. Italian Seasoning 2 c. sliced zucchini (I just use 2 small zucchini's) 1- 6 oz. can sliced black olives (drained) 1 pkg. Cheese Tortellini 1 c. carrots diced 1 can kidney beans Grated Parmesan Cheese	1. In large sauce pot, heat oil on medium heat, add in sausage and brown links whole. 2. Add garlic and onion. After onion is tender and sausage is cooked, drain grease and slice sausage. 3. Return sliced sausage, to pot and add beef broth, water, garlic, onion mixture, tomatoes (drained), Italian seasoning, carrots, zucchini and beans. 4. Let simmer for 20 min or until zucchini is tender. 5. Approx. 10 minutes prior to dinnertime add tortellini and olives. Cook until tortellini is tender, approx. 8-10 min. 6. Serve in bowls, top with parmesan cheese.

CREATE YOUR OWN MEAL PLAN!

To use the create your own meal planner:

1. Print the blank monthly planning calendar on cardstock and laminate.
2. Hang the calendar on your refrigerator. If you do not have a magnetic refrigerator, I suggest using magnetic laminate for your monthly planning sheet (laminate on the front and magnetic material on the back).
3. Print the meal labels on cardstock, then laminate with magnetic laminate. You can either print my pre-labeled meal stickers and/or make your own with the blank sheet provided! (If you can't find magnetic laminate, you can also use the magnetic adhesive sheets and place a small magnet on the back of each label sticker.)
4. Cut apart the labels, then add them to your planner as desired.

Monthly Meal Plan for: _____

SUNDAY	MONDAY	TUESDAY	WEDNESDAY	THURSDAY	FRIDAY	SATURDAY

Copyright © 2016 Erica Made Designs, LLC

Meal Plan Labels:

Print on cardstock, write in your own meal ideas, then laminate and place a magnet on the backside.
Arrange as desired on the blank menu plan calendar.

Breakfast	Snacks	Lunch	Lunch	Dinner	Dinner
Green Smoothie	Creamy Dill Dip	Chicken Nuggets	Lunchables	BBQ Ribs	Hot Taco Soup
Smoothies	Creamy Ranch Dip	Pizza Bites	Italian Sandwich	Beef Brisket	Beef Pot-Roast
Granola Bars	Cinnamon Chips	Fish Sticks	Pasta Salad	Beef Burritos	Lasagna Roll-Ups
Pancakes	Christmas Trees	Hot Dogs	Homemade Lunchabl	Breaded Chicken	Meatloaf
Muffins	Fruit Salsa	Grilled Cheese	Tortilla Wraps	Calzones	Mongolian Beef
Fruit	Orange Salad	Grilled Turkey	Fruit Salad	Cheese/Broccoli Soup	Penne Pasta
FrenchToast	Peppermint Bark	Chicken Salad	Tomato Soup	Chicken Parmesan	Pork Roast
Yogurt	Pizzelles	Mac-n-Cheese	PB & Honey Sandwich	Chicken Stir-Fry	Sloppy Joes
Bagels	Soft Pretzels	Bologna Sandwich	PB & Banana Sandwich	Coconut Chicken	Spanish Rice
Eggs/Toast	Popcorn	PB&J		Chicken Burritos	Spiral Ham
Cottage Cheese	Grapes	Grilled Ham/Cheese		Rotisserie Chicken	Stuffed Shells
Egg, Ham & Cheese Bagels	Cheese/Crackers	Hamburgers		Enchilada Casserole	Pork Chops
Yogurt/Granola	Apples/Peanut Butter	Mini Pizzas		Fajitas	Tater-Tot Casserole
Cereal	Veggies/Dip	Pinwheels		Green Chili	Tortellini Soup
Oatmeal	Graham Crackers	Egg Salad		Ham/Bean Soup	Taco Salad
	Trail Mix	Tuna Salad		Homemade Pizza	Quesadilla

Meal Plan Labels:

Print on cardstock, write in your own meal ideas, then laminate and place a magnet on the backside. Arrange as desired on the blank menu plan calendar.

Pink (Snacks)	Green (Meals)	Green (Meals)
Granola Bar	BBQ Chicken	Grilled Chicken
White Choc. Popcorn	Spaghetti	Sweet/Sour Pork Chop
Gogurt	Polska Kielbasa	Breaded Chicken
Parfait	Ravioli	BBQ Brats
Hot Chocolate	Rigatoni	Ham/Bean Soup
Graham Crackers	Italian Pot Roast	Beef Burritos
PB & Honey Sandwich	Pork Chops	Lasagna Roll-Ups
Cheese Cubes	Chicken Parmesan	
Pretzels	Enchiladas	
Chex Mix	Beef Stroganoff	
Christmas Trees	BBQ Pork	
Munchie Platter	Hamburgers	
String Cheese	Chicken Burritos	
	Meatloaf	
	Grilled Steak	
	Lettuce Wraps	

Blank Meal Plan Labels:

Print on cardstock, write in your own meal ideas, then laminate and place a magnet on the backside. Arrange as desired on the blank menu plan calendar.

Made in the USA
Monee, IL
12 March 2022